A NEW DAY IS DAWNING

A Powerful New Message From Jesus For Your Life Today And The Future Of Our Planet

Communicated Through

INWARD JOURNEY PUBLISHING
NAPERVILLE, ILLINOIS
www.inwardjourney.com

Inward Journey Publishing
P.O. Box 6418
Naperville, IL 60567-6418
1-888-980-5780

P.O. Box 239
Sedona, AZ 86339-0239

FIRST EDITION, 1997

Library of Congress Catalog Card Number: 95-82254

ISBN 1-888473-87-8
Printed in the United States of America.
10 9 8 7 6 5 4 3

Contents

Acknowledgments

Along the path of life there are many people that shape our destiny and without whom we would not accomplish our goals in life.

This book is one such accomplishment. There are many who have encouraged me along the way. To all of those my heartfelt thanks. You know who you are.

There are, however, some fellow sojourners in life that without their work and support this beautiful message might not have found its way into your hands. I wish to thank Lynn & Sam Tardio and Patricia for your unwavering support in producing this book. My thanks to Donna Wozniak and Mary Montgomery-Clifford for your hours spent in helping to format the layout. My gratitude to Clarence Deigel, Jody Edholm, Doug Jensen, Betty Parks, Peggy Parsegian, Judy Scheffres, Shirley Skillin, Karin Stenaae, and Linda Wittenberg for your support along the way. To all those that participated in these beautiful visits from Jesus, asking your questions to clarify the message Jesus was giving, I thank you.

There is one very special person to whom I must express my gratitude, Batavia, my soul mate. It was his wisdom, tireless encouragement and hard work that brought this book into reality. I think Jesus must have known his words would touch deep into the heart of Batavia and that he would dedicate himself to bringing this beautiful message of hope and inspiration to the whole world. Thank you, my friend and soul mate for your belief and trust.

Most of all I give my thanks and gratitude to Jesus that through all my times of questioning and doubt you were unwavering in your love and patience bringing forth your message for today.

When I asked Jesus, "Why did you choose to communicate your message through me?" He answered with love, "You were listening."

Diandra

A Note To The Reader

I feel honored to share these visits from Jesus with you, the reader. As with many events in our lives, at the time we do not always see the end of the journey. Each choice is a stepping stone to a wider path in life.

I felt a sacred reverence and an excited anticipation as Jesus gave the guidance that his messages were to be shared with the entire world. I believe there are no accidents nor coincidences in life. If this book has found its way into your day, then I am excited for the doors it shall open in your consciousness and the great love you will feel as you move through the pages.

I believe all life is one. I believe there is not a division of thought and that communication is not limited to our belief in the physical world. Opening to this awareness has been a very real and life changing experience that I share with others.

I invite you to share your experiences with me and others as you read this beautiful and uplifting message from Jesus for your life today. I believe many are being called to step forward in this time of transition on our planet. Perhaps you feel, as I do, the great love that is given to our planet. Perhaps you feel compelled to share your love with others. Perhaps you are one who will choose to dedicate your life to the healing of our world.

In the words of Jesus, "A new day is dawning," and we all share in this time of awakening. My love to you.

—  Diandra

Introduction

There was a man called Jesus. Many beliefs and much mystery surround his birth, life and death. Some say he was a great teacher, prophet and master soul. Some say he was God Incarnate on Earth. As a devoted follower of Christ from early childhood, he was my Lord and Savior. I have since come to know this great soul in a deeper, much more profound way. His love is beyond my ability to convey. His gentleness, kindness and compassion for all souls is more than I can comprehend. I have come to intimately know his beautiful energy through his many visits to convey his message for today.

He has taught me a greater love than I knew we could give to one another. Upon his request, and with Jesus always by my side, these beautiful visits from Jesus are shared with you. This is Jesus' message to the world today.

As you read the words, know that Jesus is there with you. If you have questions, ask him to bring clarity and understanding to the message. Most of all, open yourself to feel his great love as you share in his words.

PART I

A Powerful New Message From Jesus For Your Life Today

Journey with me down your path of light, and I will be faithful in staying with you. Walk with me down the dusty roads, and we will bring light to heal the pain. We will do it together.

— Jesus

CHAPTER 1

The Parable

*I will tell you a story that is
not unlike your own life.*

Imagine yourself walking down a dusty road.
Beautiful green olive trees line one side. Lush green
meadows and rolling hillsides extend in the distance
as far as your eyes can see. There are other travelers on the
road, some have come from a great distance while others
live in the nearby village. You greet one another as you
pass. As you round a bend in the road looking into the distance, there on a hillside you see a crowd sitting listening
to a man as he speaks with arms outstretched.

There is a hushed silence among those on the hillside
that invites you to join the assembly.

As you climb the gentle slope, you hear his voice even
before you are near. You wonder how can it be that his
voice is so clear at such a distance.

You hear this man in a gentle yet compelling voice say,
I will tell you a story that is not unlike your own life. Again
the silence of wonder falls over the crowd as the words
come forth. You find a shady spot in which to sit and join
the men, women and children on the hillside. As you listen,
Jesus' love and compassion touches your heart as he begins
to speak—

The Parable Begins

This is Jesus. I would like to tell you the story of a very great and wise King. This King ruled over all the known land with great love. His subjects had all they needed or desired. They had no worries. They were never hungry nor cold. They were given spacious homes filled with elaborate furnishings and decorations, fine clothing and plenty of food. All was beautiful.

Life was very good. Then one day the King said perhaps I should allow the people to begin to choose for themselves; perhaps I am restricting them by taking such care of them. Maybe they should begin to choose how they wish to care for themselves. So he gave equal portions of land, clothing and means of exchange to all subjects and said, "You now choose how you wish to live your life, what you wish to do and how you wish to interact with each other, for I feel that perhaps I have not allowed you the freedom that you needed to truly be as great as you can be. You look to me and believe that I am so great, and yet, you are just as great as I. Maybe I have not allowed you to achieve your own greatness, so all the things that you now look to me to provide I give to you. You now know you are as great as I. You no longer have a need to look to me for your good; you can sustain all that you desire for yourself."

In the beginning, the subjects were delighted with this new found power and freedom. They recognized they, indeed, could create for themselves all the beautiful things they desired. While they still loved and adored their King, they no longer had to be dependent upon the King, for they knew they were powerful and free. They had all the things the King possessed. As time went by, the people had less contact with their King. The gracious and loving giver of life began to slip into the background. The people's memory of their beloved King began to fade.

Soon the people began to forget the regal qualities that were given to them as a natural birthright. They had no image to guide them. Without the visible direction of their King, they forgot who they were. They now believed they were separated from their King, separated from their source of good and separated from what they had always known. The open, harmonious communication among the people no longer existed. They began to believe there was something else they must do to sustain the qualities given them to have this greatness of which the King had spoken. As they began to search outside themselves to find where these great qualities came from, they began to think the qualities were no longer there, and maybe they would run out of whatever it was that sustained their good. Maybe they should plan a way of taking their neighbors goods while they could. This created conflict.

As conflict grew, no one felt safe any longer. When they no longer felt safe, they built walls and fortresses. People gathered in small and large groups. They pooled their goods together within their groups to sustain and to protect themselves. Groups attacked other groups and tore down their walls to gather more goods to feel safe. The many separate groups expanded their conflict into raging wars. As eons passed, the people laid to devastation all that was beautiful and good. They no longer remembered their own, inner power or how their existence began in the first place. They no longer felt the King was there, although he was.

They sank deeper and deeper into a life of pain, fear and struggle. The people's goods became scattered. Those people who became skilled took from others; some people had many goods while others had none. Some people inflicted pain on others while others received pain. The receivers of pain then grew stronger and returned the pain. As generations died and as generations were born, they all forgot totally the gift the King had given them. They didn't even know the gift was there. All they knew was to take goods, protect themselves and to give as they felt it was safe to give.

And so it is with humanity. I would come and live and die again if it would free just you, but it will not. Do not seek your salvation from without; it is within yourself. It has already been given to you. Open to your Spirit and soul; remember who you are. You are God expressing. If you will open your heart and soul, I will share with you.

You ask me how long before humanity will heal their pain? Oh my beloved, I ask you the same question. *How long before humanity will heal their pain? How long before you return to the King and remember all the gifts you were given?* Your walls are built, and they are torn down. You inflict and receive pain, but when you cease to inflict pain, you will no longer receive pain. You do not remember you have everything you need to fulfill your desires. How long before you remember all the gifts you were given? How do you rediscover that awareness?

You find it first by stopping the pain; stop inflicting pain and stop receiving pain.

If there were something more I could do, do you not think I would do it? You must choose to heal your pain through love. I extend to you all my Love, the Love of the Creator and the Holy Spirit which is the reality of Love that abides in your Spirit, reaching into your soul.

- Suggested Meditation -
High Pasture
Page 133

CHAPTER 2

Jesus' Time And Purpose On Earth
- A Clarification -

When I walked your planet as the man called Jesus,
I taught the people as best they could understand
at the time, but souls have evolved.

This is Jesus. I enter your presence from the Love of the Creator. I desire to begin by giving clarity to my role in history. My incarnation was for the sole purpose of showing you the way home. I came that you might have a visible portrait of the human soul as lived through the divinity of your Spirit.

All that exists is God expressing God. When the Creator sent forth the spark of life, that one divine thought contained within itself the totality of all life. Your soul is no different from my soul. It is only your limited awareness of who you are that is different. For eons of time your soul has traveled many paths and experienced many levels of consciousness. I would say to you, *if you had not always retained the awareness of your divinity, you would not be listening to my words.*

It is this awareness hidden deep within your consciousness I wish to fully awaken. When I came to your planet as Jesus, I came to show the people a loving God. I came to teach you that you too are Love. You have this Love buried so deep within the frightened ego personality you do not remember who you are. You are an extension and expression of an omnipotent and loving Creator. You are the co-creator of your world. All that exists, exists within you. You are All That Is.

When I came to your planet, I stayed for only a brief time. I chose all the learning experiences your planet offered that I might understand humanity. I did extensive traveling that I might learn from those who had the greatest insight of the time, those that were dedicated to bringing balance to humanity. I also chose those souls that I had need of to be the closest to me. For when you are serving others, it is important your own inner circle be those who are going to enhance your efforts.

The energy of fear and illusion on your planet is heavy, often making the physical a challenging experience.

If you have chosen a task to do, you need the support of those who are of like energy. If you surround yourself by those who would negate all you attempt to do, I would say to you, you've created a nearly impossible situation for yourself.

I speak to you as though you are going to change the world because you are. How quickly and how great the change depends upon how much you allow your spiritual nature to express through the frightened ego personality which is entrenched in the belief of its own illusion. You change the world every day. You may not receive great acclaim for having done so, and you may not even be aware of it, but every day you do change the world. Those you touch are changed, and those they touch are changed.

When I walked your planet as the man called Jesus, I taught the people as best they could understand at the time, but souls have evolved. Your consciousness has expanded, your understanding is clearer, and today my teachings can be better understood. You can listen with an awareness that humanity did not have 2,000 years ago.

Yet, it was the perfect time. If I were to come today in physical form and give you the same teachings, they would not be kept in as pure a form as they were kept at that time. Your world communications are extremely vast. Your interpretation of truth is so distorted that by the time it reaches the masses it would not retain the degree of purity of my teachings of 2,000 years ago. Even though the people at that time did not totally understand my teachings, they shared what they understood with others.

Let us now talk about my life on your planet. When I was born on your planet, it was by choice, and it was in simplicity. I lived as you live and felt as you feel. I felt all the emotions of humanity, but I understood them from the perfection and reality of Love. In that awareness, a soul is able to integrate the reality of all it truly is with who it has chosen to be. In that integration somewhere is found a balance that says, "I am not quite what I appear to be, for I am not all that I can be." My purpose was to help you to recognize the all that you can be.

As I spoke to the masses, it was not so often the words that I spoke, but it was the love they felt that made the impact upon their souls. They realized there were more than just words being spoken, because words are totally inadequate. Your vocabulary is so limited that true communication must also reach from soul to soul.

You must remember, when I came to your planet I entered

a society that believed God was a vengeful, punishing God. Thus, there were many rules to follow creating undue burdens that were laid upon the people. As I taught and walked among the masses, they felt the lightness, beauty, strength and purity of the reality of Love. My presence on the planet was to demonstrate a God of Love. Your Creator loves you.

Love is All That Is was a totally new concept. It was too radical a departure from what was known. Humanity understood living with boundaries and following rules because people seem to need the self-imposed limitations to feel comfortable. God does not impose limitations; you do. Therefore, as the teachings went forth, the limitations went forth as well. The groups that formed together once again placed limitations and rules on all the words that were given. Once again humanity chose the self-imposed, structured, defined, way of life that they knew, instead of the freedom of Love.

The time is now coming when rules will no longer serve you. Although humanity believes rules are needed when a soul is experiencing in the physical form, I would ask you to lay aside the rules of your religious beliefs in order that together we might reach a greater truth. This truth is the reality of creation. You are created in the reality of Love, your soul and Spirit are one with All That Is.

God as Physical Form

How are you able to express your total reality in a physical world with so many beliefs of limitation? Physical existence is a complex expression of God. It feels so limiting. Physical is a dense vibration, and yet, there is great beauty.

Your creations and your thought processes go on forever, but when you are not in physical form, you can change them very quickly. Accomplishing this change while in physical is much more difficult. When I was in physical form, I felt your limitation of being physical. You, my friends, feel the limitations of physical but do not have the conscious awareness of the limitations. Deep inside you know you are unlimited, and yet, you are bound by your own perception of limitation.

As you create in your third-dimensional physical form, know everything you are creating in physical form is being created in a nonphysical world as well. One day you will have the opportunity to see all your creations in a nonphysical world without the perceptions of your physical nature. That is when you are going to appreciate the beauty of what you have created.

It will be the time when you will reap the rewards of your life on Earth. At that time you are going to understand the peace, the balance and the harmony of the oneness of all life that you do not presently understand while experiencing physical form on this planet.

I now speak to you of the crucifixion and the resurrection.

The crucifixion was a necessary public event, and the resurrection was the evidence you are an immortal soul.

Again, you must recall at the time I came, many of those to whom I came felt there was not life beyond death. Had I not experienced a public death, there would have been questions of the resurrection. My resurrection was no more than the transformed body that you, too, shall have.

Humanity has not quite reached the stage of remembering how to do this, but you are rapidly awakening to that remembrance. You are now sustaining the body by substitution of body parts. You are beginning to recognize that the body is only matter placed together in a very slow vibrational form. It is much like a piece of equipment that you are exchanging worn out parts for new ones. Growing in your realization of vibrational form, you are also going to recognize the body does not need to decay.

What are you going to do with your body when you once again fully recognize vibrational form? Are you going to choose to live in your present body for an eternity, or are you going to choose transformation to a higher vibration in which you are not encumbered by the present vibration of physical? As you begin to recognize your creative power at the energy level of matter, you will go through a transformation process that will return your physical form to a state of perfection.

You will then be expressing the perfection that you truly are in your physical form. You will begin to realize you are not your physical body. That, my friends, is when you will recognize you are a part of your Creator and not separated from your God. That is when your planet will once again express physical form in all of the perfection that you are. You will once again come to play on the beautiful playground of planet Earth. You will leave at will and then return to play again and again. Death will not be needed to leave the planet. Rather you will increase the third-dimensional, denser vibrational rate of your physical body to a much higher frequency thereby causing freedom from the gravitational and energy pull of Earth. Your body will become etheric as you leave your beautiful, physical world behind, only to once again return your consciousness to the physical at another moment of thought.

You are on your way home and on your way to recognizing your true nature. As you stepped down your energies, became physical and forgot the reality of who and what you were, you became enmeshed in all your creations of ego, personality and limited mental capacities. You believed that was who you were. There now are those souls who are beginning to recognize with a certainty and a truth, these creations of egos, personalities and analytical minds are only a reflection of vibrational form and not truly who they are.

At any moment you choose to remember the perfection of who you are, you will be able to transform all that you presently are and all that is around you.

It does not matter the steps I would give you to take if you do not remember who you are. If I cannot help you to have the awareness of your true reality of Love, all the words I say to you are hollow, empty and meaningless because they do not fit the ego, they do not fit the personality and they are not understood by your analytical mind. They are understood by your divine mind that is a part of All That Is.

You must listen to my words from your heart. The words will not make a difference in your life if they are only reaching the analytical, mental consciousness, for the mind will reject my words as improper data. The words have no meaning to the mind because the mind has no past experiences upon which to base the words.

You must go within to your soul and Spirit. As you receive revelation from within, you glimpse the greatness, the wonder and the beauty of who you are, that will then begin to manifest itself in your daily life. This gives the mind an experience to analyze and then ACCEPT. You cannot reach this inner truth through the analytical mind that your own ego created, nor can that mind create in your life the greatness and wonder of your Spirit. To reach your inner truth, you must go beyond your mind and allow the truth of who you are to flow into your life. The consistent use of meditation in your life opens a powerful doorway to go beyond the mind into your Spirit.

Q: When you walked this Earth, did you have to go through the same process everyone is going through now in order to come to the knowledge of truth?

At the time I walked this Earth as Jesus, I was enlightened. I had experienced the Earth many times but never in the capacity that you are thinking. Let me explain.

You have had what you have come to know as the enlightened ones that have come to your planet. Their souls have not spent a great amount of time on your planet in previous existences, and they have not become as entrapped in all of the illusion as have many other souls.

All souls make choices and the enlightened souls made particular choices that kept their path purer and clearer than many other souls. Thus, they are not as entrapped and therefore, do not have the same path as souls that have allowed the illusion to become their reality. This all began when God had a thought which sent forth a stream of energy creating a soul.

It all was and is a matter of a soul's many choices. Each one of those sparks could have chosen to remain in the pure reality of creation. As the individual souls began to create, they realized their ability of creative power as it affected their own soul and others. Souls became entangled in the creation process.

As the souls became entangled in the creation process, it was as though they became what they had created. The souls believed they were their creations rather than the creator; the reality of who they were was forgotten. However, there remain those souls who have not become entrapped by their creations as have many other souls. These souls have not only incarnated on your planet in your life form, but they've often gone to other worlds and many other existences. They are the enlightened masters, the teachers and the healers for other worlds as well.

There are those souls that have never incarnated on Earth and have stayed in the awareness of reality. Those souls having never chosen to be physical do not struggle with the same illusion as does humanity.

Those souls that remained in the awareness of reality have their own path to follow. Other existences have their own forms of their creations, their refinements, their experiencing and their own journey to explore.

I did not incarnate as you incarnate today. I had a clearer awareness of the reality of life and the consciousness of Love. I was not entrapped by the fears and illusions of your world. You do not need to be entrapped in them either. Some souls are more entrapped in the illusion than others. For some, it will take moving a mountain range to free them. For others, stripping away layers will open the door to reality and for still others the need is only to pull back a curtain. Individual soul choices through many lifetimes determine how real the illusion is to each person.

As each soul chooses the reality of Love, those souls are healing the mass consciousness and clearing the path for others. It is easier now to remember reality than a few years ago. You are, indeed, changing the structure and existence on your planet. You are awakening.

You can recognize the souls who are healing the illusion as you come into their presence. When you feel unconditional, nonjudgmental love, you are in the presence of one who moves toward enlightenment, a soul that is choosing to awaken. Take advantage of their presence to heal your own pain of illusion.

Q: In the Bible you told us that we would do even greater things than those that you did when you were here on this earthly plane. How can this be since you and I and all are Love but you have perfected that Love while we are still trying to get to that point? So, then, how can there by anything greater than the Love you were when you manifested here in the physical? How can we do greater than that?

When I came into your world as the man Jesus, I was not a part of mass consciousness. I incarnated through a very pure stream of energy that knew its own power. From the moment this energy stream entered the womb, there was total awareness—the same awareness that I am saying to you to remember. My life was lived from total awareness. I chose to experience this planet, but those experiences did not limit my interaction with your world because I was consciously aware I was God.

What greater things can you do than I? Heal yourself. I could not heal the world. I could show humanity who they are and their possibilities. I could love them and live among them. I could share and teach, but I could not heal the world.

As each person heals himself or herself, that individual helps the world to heal. I could not effect the mass consciousness because I was not a part of the mass consciousness. What I taught to others and how they used it, effected mass consciousness. They did a greater deed than I because they effected mass consciousness.

It is not through the outside social reforms you heal your world. Those reforms may last a millennium, a few hundred years or maybe less. When your soul truly effects a healing change within yourself, you effect it for every lifetime you have ever lived and shall live in your future. Time is part of the illusion. In reality there is no time. Your healing affects all those with whom you have interacted. You affect all the generations born from the first time your soul entered the planet, and you affect future generations.

When you move into your spiritual awareness, there is a realization of the nonexistence of time. Therefore, as you heal yourself, you know the genes and cellular memory are being effected without the limitation of time.

As you begin to become aware of who you are without questioning and doubting but desiring to truly move into your power, one of the first signs is humility. Humility is the ingredient that says I have caught the wonder of life and existence, and it is so vast and beautiful I need not exalt myself in the presence of my friends nor my enemies. When you reach this point, you have begun to heal.

When I say the word exalt, I mean you feel your presence must be made known and perhaps be shown to be greater than another. This is done in many ways. A little child has an equal presence in your world as any adult but is not always given respect because the physical child is unable to defend itself. You, however, are able to exalt yourself with the child, and the child is unable to bring you down. When you can exalt yourself with those who are weaker than you, it makes you feel safe. Look at the ways you exalt yourself.

When you have no need for exaltation, you are on your path to healing. Others will then exalt you, but it will not mean anything to you. They exalt you because they feel the presence of the true power that lies within you, for they are in search of this same power. It is a power that literally can say to the mountain, "Move into the sea," and the mountain will move, for there are no boundaries or limitations to your power. Your true reality as an expression of God is not the person you now know yourself to be; it is not the you that you think you are, but rather you are an unlimited expression of an unlimited Creator.

So when you ask me the question how can you do greater things than I, in response I ask you the question, *how could you not do greater things than I?* You have so much more opportunity.

- Suggested Meditation -
The Light Of Love
Page 135

CHAPTER 3

Honor And Love Yourself
As You Are

I wish you to know the beauty of humanity.
Look for the inner beauty in all life.
See the greatness that lies within.

I bring to you the Love of the Creator and the blessings of the universe. I take this Love and I impregnate it into your heart that through the heart you might allow it to journey to the mind. It is as though I am able to share with you a glimpse of true awareness of the Love, the beauty and the brilliance that you are. Take that small grain of awareness and allow it to germinate manifesting beauty that radiates in your physical creations.

Your Soul

If you wonder how well you are doing on planet Earth, look into the radiance coming through your eyes. The eyes are the mirror of your soul. When you question how well your soul is listening to the guidance of your Spirit, look at the radiance in your eyes. If your eyes, my friends, are sad, then know you are not allowing the beauty of your reality to express. If your eyes are laughing, that is wonderful because laughter is a healing medicine. If your eyes are dancing and sparkling, then know your soul is expressing love.

The soul reflects the totality of your creations from the time the Creator emitted the spark of energy that was to become your individual expression. Your soul is so beautifully, uniquely the expression of the totality of you. Allow your Spirit, the God-essence within you, to radiate through your soul that your beauty might shine through the physical body.

The reality of your Love perfects your physical. The body cannot be perfected from without. Perfection of the body occurs when you allow the perfection of your Spirit to radiate through the physical. Allow the perfect Love of the Creator to radiate through your soul into your physical, emotional and mental bodies bringing peace and harmony to all that touches your life.

Be Love

My one request to you today is, be Love. Be what you are, the very energy, the very essence of your Creator. Be Love. Allow love to enfold all that you touch. Create from love, and the beauty of love will radiate around you.

There are those who would say to me, "How can I take the message to others?" You do not take the message. You are the message. Whatever you are is the message you are sharing. If the words you speak are not in harmony with your thoughts and emotions, you send a message of confusion and conflict.

I speak to you by vocabulary because it is how you are familiar with communications. The vocabulary has little lasting impact. It is the soul communication we share that will last. Soul communication will make the words come alive within you. As souls blend together, all the reality of their creations recognize the reality of the Spirit, creating the harmony and the music of the universe.

Love one another. Be good to one another. Love those that you perceive to be your enemies for they are not. Be good to them. They are in pain, and they are you. All life is one.

Give love to the souls who have gone on and are no longer in the physical, for they also journey a path. Love is the answer.

In these visits I could say so many things to you, but it wouldn't matter unless somehow I could convey to you love.

I extend to you the Love of the Creator. The Holy Spirit is the Love that reaches into your Spirit—awakening the Love within you. The angels serve you. There is such love for your world, but how can I help you to love you?

See the star of Bethlehem. Feel the essence of the star of Bethlehem, for it shines bright on your planet. It is a guiding light. Look very carefully and you shall see signs and wonders but perhaps not as you thought they would be. Look for the little things—the little miracles, and as your faith and trust increases, so shall the miracles. Go forth with courage, strength and in truth. Wrap it all in love, and you shall find that which you seek. I come to you from the Love of the Father (the Creator), the Son (Humanity) and the Holy Spirit (the Love and life force of the Universe).

Honor Yourself

I honor mankind. I say to you, honor yourself as you are in the present moment, for, you see, in your judgments of your human race, you hold yourself in bondage. Bondage was never intended to be a part of the creative process on your world. You have the most beautiful playground of all creation. You have been given the most elaborate tools to have the experiences of your choosing. But, it seems, instead, you have formed for yourself an arena of judgment that holds you in the bondage of your judgments.

I did not come to judge your world. Much to the contrary belief of some of humanity, I shall never judge your world. For what is there to be accomplished in judgments? Judgments only set about to entrap you in a behavioral pattern that seems to be too difficult to change.

You have the need to evaluate and understand your experiences upon your planet. You set your judgments in motion, keeping alive the energy which creates yet another similar experience. Judgment is a strong energy of bondage to yourself, others and your planet.

As the masters and teachers have come to your world, it has never been to establish more judgments nor to inflict more laws or rules. It has always been to show you that within yourself lies all possibilities of creative experience.

I come to you only as your brother and say to you, *although you may never entertain an angel in a physical sense nor see the masters who walk among you, our presence is very, very near.* I wish to be here only to help show you the way to lift from yourself the heaviness you seem to self-impose lifetime after lifetime.

You impose burdens upon yourselves which are heavy to bear. Burdens are lifted when you choose instead to see the beauty in all existence.

Look into the soul of all existence, whether it is a flower, a blade of grass or a gaze upward into the sky. Feel the existence of the stars in the sky during the day, not only during the night. Look for the inner beauty in all life. See the greatness within all existence.

Shallow thoughts and views of the surface only allow you to interact with judgments of the past. You must go beyond learned behavior to move into the inner beauty of life.

I wish you to know how much you are loved. I wish you to know how Love sets you free. I wish you to know how abundantly rich is the process of life in your universe. I wish you to know the beauty of humanity.

The Expression Of Love

There are no words which can convey to you the true expression of Love that exists between all souls. This is something you must find for yourself. As you begin to reach out with your love, you connect with the love in others.

As you walk among humanity in your world, it is your choice to see each soul's pain or to see each soul's beauty. As you see the beauty, you bring forth the beauty. It is so easy for your ego, which feels alone and threatened, to connect to the frightened ego in another who also feels alone, threatened and in pain. Although you may find a moment of personal satisfaction in feeding the pain that exists in others, it is but a brief moment of satisfaction. It is a satisfaction only to the pain that exists within you.

As you choose to relate to the pain in another, you amplify the pain in you. Pain validates illusion as there is no pain in reality. Your ego is in pain and fear, for it is unaware of the reality you are. Therefore, if you do not remember who you truly are, then by validating the illusion, you reassure yourself "you exist." If you will but go beyond the pain you find in your brothers and sisters and look beyond the actions the pain activates in their lives, you would see instead the great beauty within their souls. Then you would find the same beauty within yourself. You discover the oneness that is all life. You have found a force of comradeship binding you and other souls. The person who seemed to be so at odds with you becomes an ally.

The Children

I wish to address the children for a moment. Your children are in great turmoil, for they are lacking in the parental love that has been their guide. This is because your own souls have become so encased within your own pain it has become difficult for you to survive; therefore, your survival alone requires all of your energy. Very little energy remains to give to the children of your world. The children are left to find their own way through the maze of conflict, often with little support.

Many enlightened souls have returned. They are often the little children on your planet. They have come to teach you love is still the reality of life.

Many children give their lives willingly as you inflict your pain upon them whether it is in your war-torn cities or whether it is emotional, mental or physical abuse.

Many souls incarnate in the hope their love will reach into your hearts and somehow help you to heal. As little children, they put their arms around your neck for they have so much love to share, but you do not have the time to receive their love. When they see there is nothing they can do to help souls heal, they often find a way to escape your world and return to their nonphysical existence.

I say to you, *reach out as a child and love in the innocence of a child, that you might rise from your own despair and your own struggle of life again remembering what is important.* Remembering all life is one. Remembering all life contains the same elements of divinity. It is only how you choose to express divinity and how your perceptions of pain from your own experiences hide your awareness of divinity that dictates the journey of your soul.

Feel the power of your own love and be willing to share that love with another and with your hurting world. Until your brother and sister are healed, humanity as a whole will not forsake one single soul, for indeed, you are your brother's keeper, and indeed, your brother is your keeper. All life exists as one.

All life sings as one song thereby composing the music

of the universe. Listen carefully—and you will understand the melody of life.

I send to you my brothers and sisters the only gift I have to give and that is my Love. It is the sharing of love that is the way to your salvation, for in the sharing of love you find your own reality of Love. You are the way, you are the truth, and you are the life. You shall find your way to your own divinity.

Q: You say we are to honor ourselves, do we not do this when we honor another, or is it that we must first honor ourselves before we are capable of honoring another? And, how do we honor ourselves?

Let us first of all define honor in the context to be understood by your consciousness. Honor means simply to have a recognition of the totality of all that you are and All That Is—recognizing the totality. You see, you are willing to recognize bits and parts of who you are and bits and parts of others. You are willing to recognize what you consider the beauty of all elements whether that is in nature, another person or yourself. But when you honor, you honor the totality of an existence.

The totality of an existence means you must embrace all you are aware of in that existence. You must not deny honor to any. Humanity is very good at denial. Deep within yourself you bury those things you feel are too cumbersome, too burdensome, too much to deal with, or that are too overwhelming. This is not honoring, for you see you must honor the part of yourself you feel is the most difficult. Honor in another person what irritates you the most. When you can honor those things, it means you can embrace them.

Now, what do I mean by embrace? It means you can allow all things to be a part of your existence without denial,

accepting the harmony in all things, the joy in any existence and the beauty in that which you have deemed not
beautiful.

Honoring is to bow at the knee of one you feel has been
the most difficult. Honoring is exalting the least among you.
Honoring is to say to what appears to be a thorn in your
side, "I embrace the thorn and all of its beauty." It is very
easy to use the word honor when it fits into your life as
something you feel is beneficial and beautifies anything
around you. But that is not the way I use the word honor. I
use the word honor to embrace the totality of all.

How can you embrace the totality of that which you feel
is outside of yourself if you do not embrace it within yourself? You see it is not just without but it is within. So it is a
commonalty of embracing All That Is, both within and without.

How do you do that? You do it by removing your judgments; you do it by allowing yourself to come to a place of
trust, faith and safety in your existence. You do it by believing there is a power within you sustaining your existence
through all dimensions, through all space and all time, for
the only thing you truly fear is your cessation of existence.
If you can believe in your existence, that it is safe and that
it cannot be extinguished, then you can honor yourself and
all other things. Only then can you embrace all things in
your existence and know nothing can harm or destroy your
existence in any way.

**Q: Jesus, you talked about choices—it is our choice
to see each soul's pain or to see each soul's beauty. When
you walked on the planet, did anyone ever physically
threaten you, and if they did, how did you transform
that? Many times in our world we feel physically threatened, and I wonder how best to deal with that?**

The answer to your question has two parts. First of all, the physical was not something I feared would not exist. So without the fear I could not be threatened, for you see what is there to threaten if a threat does not create fear? I knew physical existence was a state of consciousness, and I recognized physical existence was not my destiny for a long period of time. I also knew my consciousness would maintain physical existence until the time I would choose to release the physical, life form. This is true for you, my friends. The difference is you do not have the awareness that your physical existence shall maintain its state of consciousness until the time your soul is ready to release it. Thus, you have a fear it can be threatened or harmed in some way.

Second, I would say to you my physical existence did come to a physical harm, as you think of physical harm, on your planet. But I would also say to you I chose to allow the event. I chose to allow and embrace the pain my physical body encumbered and because it was a choice, it was not threatening nor fearful. The only reason the event took place was because it was a human experience I chose.

> *My death could have been in many ways,*
> *but it needed to be public to show that the*
> *Spirit would be triumphant, as in the*
> *resurrection.*

If you had the demonstration of the pain and the agony as humanity knew it to be, there would be no question that death would follow. I allowed the event, and therefore, I did not consider death to be a threat to my physical existence. Nothing truly can threaten you, but you feel threatened because the fear within you feels threatened.

- Suggested Meditation -
Creating With Love
Page 145

CHAPTER 4

Understanding The True Wonder of Your Existence

You are the creator, and through your creations you realize all the uniqueness and wonder of who you are. You remember you are God expressing.

This is Jesus. I speak to you of your existence. I say to you that you exist. Among all the illusions you have created, you do exist. Very little of which you are aware of around you has any substance. It is an illusion, but the purity and reality of who you are never changes. You are complete, total and existent.

First, when I say "existent," I want you to understand I am talking about the totality of all that you are. I am speaking about the completeness of you. The completeness of you embodies much more than you are aware. Completeness is the first concept you must recognize. Your soul is reality; therefore, you exist.

Second, you are a complete and total extension of your Creator. Therefore, all that is a part of you is a part of God, a part of a universal creative consciousness of Love. That means you are perfect and complete. Having only an infrequent glimpse of your completeness, you feel you are only a physical, individual personality functioning upon Earth, indeed, often struggling throughout your life.

I trust this time together will, at the very least, make you completely aware of who you are and that you may know everything you create becomes a part of you and will exist for eternity.

I say to you, you are eternal. To not exist can never happen to you.

You really have no choice but to exist. Although you may not have initiated the individual spark creating your individual soul, you have chosen every other thing that is now the composite of who you are, and it is eternal.

Your existence can be modified, it can be changed, and it can be enhanced, but what it cannot be is erased.

This is another point you must be completely aware of, not in the sense of guilt, pain, sin or unworthiness but from the point of understanding that what is created exists forever.

Within your mind's eye see a beautiful, tiny center of light, unique with a great sparkle. This tiny light has some miraculous qualities inside. This marvelous center of light is complete in itself, and it has the creative power to maintain its own existence, to multiply and bring about any new creation it desires. These creations become a part of the center of light as the light expands and expands. Many times the creations contain absolutely nothing that look like the tiny center of light in its original state of existence, but it was what the light chose to create. The creations became an expression of the creator and all are one. The light is you; it is your soul.

Creative Process

You are the creator, and through your creations you realize all the uniqueness and wonder of who you are. You remember you are God expressing.

You are the creative source of your world. As God sent out the thought of original creation that added to the existence of God, so you send out your own spark of light to begin the creative process that adds to your center of light. Your creations, too, began their creation process, adding the uniqueness of their creations to your individual soul.

It doesn't matter what your creation has been. It is your creation. You designed your creation as you wove each thread into the tapestry of life. You have encircled your center of light with the beautiful jewels of your creation and each one is its own unique shape, essence, substance and purpose. This pattern is uniquely you. In all of creation, there is not another you. That in itself is a wonder of creative existence.

When I say, *you are not aware of your totality and you are functioning only in one, tiny aspect of all that you are, I mean you as in an individualized soul.* You do not use all the power of your creative expression because you limit yourself with your perception of struggle in the physical upon this planet.

You are a multi-dimensional, individual expression of consciousness. This planet was intended to be a three-dimensional playground where you could place into a physical existence all the levels of consciousness that you were expressing in many dimensions. You have the ability to open the pathway into this complete total you, but how can this happen if you are not aware that it exists? By allowing your consciousness to expand, awareness is opened. It is important to take the time to quiet your analytical mind and listen to the divinity within. The instructions are within you. All that is needed is to trust and believe.

DO NOT SPEAK WHAT YOU DO NOT WANT because it is done when you speak it, every idle word. The laws of the universe do not sift through whether you mean what you say or intend it to happen. The creative process only puts it into motion.

When you become aware that your thoughts and words are the process of your creation upon this planet, you will guard your thoughts and you will speak your words more carefully. Your creations will become more refined, and you'll be happier with what is happening in your life.

You have unlimited, creative power. Creation is accomplished through the sound of thoughts and words. Sound is vibration. Vibration sets energy into motion causing a new creation to come forth. Thoughts are sound vibrations you most often do not hear in your present physical form. Know that you are using aspects of your creative power and levels of consciousness, of your existence from universes you do not yet consciously understand, to be what you are here on planet Earth today.

Knowing you are an extension of your Creator, what limits do you feel you have? What limits does your Creator have? Your only restrictions are those you place upon the soul aspect you call humanity in the physical on planet Earth. Your soul expresses with greater awareness on many other worlds but certainly not with the great unlimited potential you have on Earth.

You might ask why is it like this? As your creations on Earth took on the density of physical vibration, you began to think you were separate beings, separate from each other, your creations and your Creator. You felt restricted by physical form. Because you felt restricted by physical form, you then created death as a means of escape from the physical. Now you no longer remember how to come and play on your three-dimensional planet and leave at will because you are now caught in the heavy vibration of illusion that your frightened ego has created.

Reasons For Incarnation

Your soul recognizes, "If I'm going to incarnate on Earth, that part of my existence will be shutting the door on my awareness of my many other existences." So, why do you continue to incarnate into a physical form on Earth? Some souls come because there are things in the physical they wish to complete. Is that a command? Is it a duty? Is it even karma, as you often believe? No. It's because you would not be willing to let a part of your creation be left unhealed.

Some of humanity come to Earth just for additional experiences in the physical, perhaps an awareness they have never experienced, something they feel they can do better, or to achieve an understanding they wish to bring to their own soul or others.

Others come back to help other souls. Sometimes they

come back for that experience alone. Sometimes a soul has completed the earth cycle, but it feels, "Now, that I realize the wonder of physical existence, I'd like to once again incarnate on Earth."

Then there are those who come with a very deliberate and defined mission. It is a path from which they never stray.

There have also been those throughout all your history that have come to Earth not always awakening to the complete awareness of their path but still seeking their own mission.

I ask you, *why do you choose to incarnate on Earth time and again?* Each soul has had its own unique experience. Realize, you desire to restrict, define, explain or reason why life is as it is. The answer is to be found in the total soul experience that a soul has chosen, not only on Earth, but know that every soul has many levels of consciousness and exists in other creations and other universes.

There are other universes where the illusion is also very powerful. If your soul chose to express in such a universe, the illusion would be very real to you. It becomes very needed by you. However, in this lifetime you may desire to reach a higher spiritual plane, therefore, your soul chooses to express in a universe that allows you more conscious expansion in that area. Then you reach another plane, and you go to another universe, another planet, another experience of learning.

Now, your soul feels it is time to incarnate back on Earth to test this expansion of your soul. Earth is the physical playground where you reflect your evolution by your creations.

The more you recognize reality, realizing illusion is only the reflection of your creations, the more you have evolved.

Planetary Evolution

Your planet is ready to evolve and many souls have come to help with this change, to help others who do not understand. You have been awakening to who you are. Does this mean that you jump to the task? Just because there is an awareness does not mean you are always willing to follow through with the mission for which you came.

How does your soul awaken? There will be a stirring. There will be an unrest. There will be a knowing of something you cannot quite touch. With that, all you have to do is open yourself. You have all knowledge within you, but you are not yet aware of this knowledge. It may be very frightening to some and overwhelming to others. However, many souls will awaken and rejoice to be a part of this exciting time on Earth. Each soul will have to decide its part and how it will choose to interact within this evolution when the awareness is there. Each soul will make the choice to remain on Earth or return to nonphysical existence as the soul chooses its own path.

Live your life in peace, knowing all souls shall one day complete the journey.

Eternity—The Now Moment, The Absence Of Time And Space

I now speak to you further regarding existence.

What is eternity? What is forever and ever and ever, without ending, without beginning? It is the now moment. There is never a tomorrow, and there is not a yesterday. There is always only a NOW.

The moment of now encapsulates everything you have ever been, everything you will ever be. All exist in this moment, this now moment.

The absence of time and space may be a difficult concept for your mind to conceive.

Time and space are illusions of your own creative process.

Space is an illusion that is related to by vibrational rate. Space is perceived when your own vibration does not interact with another vibration in a state of awareness. However, there is no empty space.

You created time when you chose to live from your perception of your experience. Because you needed a linear progression to define the separateness of each experience, you created the illusion of time. Let us look at the illusion of time. There are moments when you say that time moves quickly or moments when time seems to drag on and on and on. When you feel the safest, most complete and happiest, time flies. When you are in fear or pain, time drags on endlessly. Time is related to your perception of the experience taking place in the present moment. It expands and contracts by your perception.

If enough humans chose, they could capture time. Time could be stopped for an hour, a day, or time could be accelerated to a point where it would eventually disappear completely. This is evidence indicating time is not a reality. If it were a reality, it would be fixed and could not be elastic. Time would be the same no matter what your perception of the experience.

Eternal is now; eternal is as far back as forever and as

far forward as forever. You will always be. It's all now. I know that it may seem a little difficult to grasp so why do I tell you this? I tell you this because too often **NOW** seems to be the least important thing to you. Yesterday, a year ago, when you were little, what you will do tomorrow, what you will do when you retire, or what you will do when you get rich enough is very important to you. Whatever you desire for a better tomorrow consumes your thoughts and energy. However, you too often feel what you do with this day, this hour, or this minute is not too important somehow. Yet, the now moment is everything that was yesterday and everything that is tomorrow.

Until you learn to give importance to the moment of now, you will not express the joy of that moment.

Your mind may remember a moment you knew no joy. Yet, this is not true, my friends. It is your perception of the moment that hides the joy of the very existence you are experiencing.

It is how you have trained your mind to look at the moment.

When you perceive you are the "victim" of a circumstance, you may be frightened or angry or even outraged, reacting with all the emotions you have created to defend your safety. In doing so, you are giving away your true power of safety. If instead you will choose to be the expression of God that you are in the eternal now moment, you will step into the true power of all life. You are no longer trapped by your emotions but free to change the circumstance. You will reach into the very Spirit of another soul reminding it of who it is. I tell you, my friends, most likely the other soul would no longer choose to do you harm. You are now reaching that person in the eternal part of who he or she is and that part wishes you no harm.

Even when you perceive you are living through the darkest moment, have the awareness of all you are. Know you alone are a unique and beautiful creation, that there is no other soul like you, know you are an expression of your Creator, and know you are eternal. In the moment that seems so difficult on planet Earth, recognize, "I am a unique me. I am God. I am eternal." Realize what you bring to the moment.

Entrapped In Perceptions And Judgments

Allow me to speak more about the purity of God that you are, indeed, to speak about God. All finite minds have a definition of God, of Creative Source. God is All That Is—ALL THAT IS. This then says God is also the things you do not like because God is All That Is. To exist outside of God is not possible. There is no existence without God. God is the creative intelligence maintaining All That Is. Creations exist, and they are neither good nor bad. You have a perception of creations. Because perceptions lead to judgments, you judge creations, both tangible and intangible by your own perception.

Let us look at the power of perception. For one moment bring to your mind something you think would be one of the most difficult things that could happen in your life and for each of you that probably would be different. Now let us bring to this thought the eternal uniqueness of God. Let us look at this thought a little differently.

You see, through your unique perception, the

circumstance, the person, the deed, and you then judge the same. You decide what is good, what is bad, what is okay, what is terrible, or what is wonderful. You judge it from your perception of all the experiences that the uniqueness of your soul has experienced. Therefore, what one person sees as absolutely wonderful can be very terrible from another person's perception or point of view. You judge whether you are safe or unsafe in a particular circumstance or if you would be safe if you were to be involved in a similar circumstance. You continually ask yourself, "Am I safe?"

A small child might perceive a very large stranger under new circumstances as frightening, while an adult feels perfectly safe in the stranger's presence. If there is then an interaction between this child and an adult that validates this fear, the child carries into adulthood a perception of "very large people or that set of circumstances," as unsafe, even though consciously they may not remember the experience.

You gather perceptions upon perceptions throughout your soul's existence, and you judge from these perceptions. Therein lies the illusion of the creation, and the illusion is the part you relate to most often. Yet, because all is created by an extension of a God that is eternal and is All That Is, All Is God.

The illusion is that your frightened ego does not feel safe and believes you can be destroyed. It does not know you are an eternal soul who cannot be destroyed. You relate to the belief of this illusion. Your false belief system of perceptions and judgments distort your awareness of God. Remove your judgments, heal the frightened ego, and you will once again see the purity of God and all creation.

The Meaning Of Physical Expression

Have an awareness that your life in the physical is a small reflective part of all that you are in the total expanse of the universe.

The physical is a very immediate reflection. It is a small, composite representation of all your energy. A part of your energy stream may be existing in other solar systems great distances from Earth. Expand the thinking of your conscious mind to the unlimited possibilities of creation, of the omnipotent creative process, and the vast unknown universe. Think of the possibility that your consciousness is not restricted to your known physical body. You are expanding. You may actually be saving a world somewhere. You may be focused on healing this planet. All that is taking place, everything you are doing in every aspect of your energy, becomes a reflection in your physical.

It is only the most advanced souls who choose to be physical. Physical expression is like the hub, the hub of all the spokes that go in many directions. Your creative ability is optimized in the physical. When you recognize what is happening in your physical is reflecting the totality of all that you are, you are able to quickly make adjustments, fine tune and improve your creative ability, simply because it is physical. The physical is so immediate. It has immediate consequences, and it has immediate rewards. This awareness then impacts everything you do on your planet.

If you wonder how long you've been around, how old your soul may be, or how highly evolved you are, the fact is if you were a new soul, you would not be on planet Earth. Now, you may be a newer soul to planet Earth than others, but you are not a new soul. You are an old soul that has now chosen to be physical on planet Earth. The very shape of your body, the very color of your eyes and your hair is not just a genetic code. You have built a road map into your physical bodies that you can learn how to read.

If your soul spends a lot of time on a planet or in a solar system that is energy or motion without form, you no doubt will have chosen a physical body that is of light complexion, light hair and light eyes. This choice may help you in the physical to remember there is creation that is without form or creation that is fluid. If you have chosen a darker complexion within your race, you no doubt spend a lot of your energy in universes dealing with a great amount of form and matter. It may be a translucent form, but it has a form.

You are continually choosing the creative process for the majority of your energy that is in other universes at the present time. If there are a combination of these choices, e.g. very fair complexioned with dark eyes, you have undoubtedly spent much soul time in both dimensions with and without form. The physical will always be a soul reflection. You may change some features as you are choosing to emphasize expression. You may choose to change your hair coloring, or you may become darker skinned through tanning. Your physical is a great guide to the inner you.

Your physical form on Earth reflects not only your energy pattern here but also how well you are in harmony with your other soul aspects. When there is a disturbance in your physical, emotional or mental bodies, you rush to fix the problem before you find the cause. Do you know what happens when you do that? When you attempt to realign yourself and you do not know the cause of the disturbance, it is as though you have a wound that you sew up, but you do not explore for foreign objects nor clean the wound. You do not discover the cause of the wound, and it becomes infected. If somewhere in your soul's journey there is an enormous energy out of balance, it will feed back into your physical existence that you might transform the blockage.

Your physical will tell you, "You've got things a little out of kilter." It matters not what is taking place. You can bring all into harmony by being the Love that you are.

You are making progress. However, you are not yet aware of your complete soul, the all that you are. You are thinking of yourself as a restricted physical form, restricted to planet Earth. Physical is a reflection of a vibrational rate of energy set into motion by sound. Everything on this planet is a reflection, just a beautiful, third-dimensional reflection. When you have a day that the emotions are totally out of balance, you may be doing a lot of changing and refining on another level, and it may reflect in your third-dimensional, physical being on Earth. By expanding your consciousness beyond your analytical mind, you become aware of your greatness and your expansive soul journey.

Your existence is eternal and forever expanding. Unlock the door to your own self-imprisonment to discover your reality of Love, beauty and greatness.

Your Planet Reflects You

Many people feel your planet is being destroyed by the actions of humanity. You feel threatened because from your perception if something happens to Earth, you do not have a place to live and neither do your children, your grandchildren nor your future generations.

This is the illusion. What if, just what if, the same creative powers that created this planet were to restore your beautiful planet to the pristine world you desire or perhaps created it even more beautiful than before? If you believed this would happen, would your perception be the same? Would you maybe then see your world differently? What if you knew that as humanity heals their pain, it heals and restores the beauty of the Earth. Would you think, "We have created a brand-new planet, and we now better understand our creative process?"

Your planet is a reflection of you, and this is the greater, more important concept. Because Earth is a reflection of humanity, it seems to say to you that you really haven't taken very good care of yourself. Yet, that, too, is an illusion because you've taken wonderful care of yourself.

As you view the reflections of your creative power, you simply say, "I want to do this differently. I think this would be more fun to do it like this. I wonder what the experience would be like if I did it differently?" My friends, you have expressed through many existences on many planets. Some of the planets where you have been no longer support the life forms you knew. They served their purpose in that form of existence. However, I can promise you, your planet Earth will never be destroyed as long as it has a purpose for its existence.

Q: Are you saying that we're really doing something somewhere else, but we're not doing it here? Is it just a reflection here?

You are reflecting in the physical what you are in many other energy forms. Physical gives you a high visibility to see the you that is somewhere else. Who you are in this physical body reflects a composite of all that you are in many forms, dimensions and universes. You may be refining the technology needed for a world you have no conscious awareness of in your physical form on Earth. The physical is a valuable barometer of your soul's total existence.

Since the physical is a reflection, what does that mean

to you? Know you are more than you appear to be. The fact you become aware allows you to balance and refine the energies. All the energy systems within you do not just connect to your physical. They connect to the totality that you are.

This beautiful, earthly, physical existence that you have chosen allows you to fine tune and to refine. It interacts with all that you are. When you smile, the world does smile with you—your entire world. You are constantly in motion. Your energy is an ever-changing composite of your soul's journey. There is always an interaction between your physical existence on Earth and the totality of who you are in all dimensions and universes. Choosing a physical existence allows you more complexity because of the strength of the density of energies in your physical form.

If it were possible for your soul to express as separate energies, which it is not—any more than you cannot separate yourself from God—it would be like operating on a flat tire. Your whole existence would be cumbersome, heavy and moving in slow motion. As you know yourself to be today, you are expressing many components of your soul that your conscious mind does not know exists.

At times the lines of energy get clogged. Do you know why this happens? The analytical, creative mind is the sentinel that is always on guard. It begins to filter out what it does not understand. It doesn't allow the energy connection to flow in the free circuitry of original intent.

Through your renewed awareness, you begin to expand your physical structure and become aware you cannot be separated from your God. In truth, you can never be separated from all of life, and you cannot be separated from all that you are. Journeying through many experiences, your soul will continue the journey of many more experiences and many more expressions of God. You begin to remember it was only a false belief by the frightened ego that you were separate and alone.

As you are awakening, you will see the beauty of your planet become even more pristine as the beauty of your bodies begin the transformation of which I spoke. Your awareness is like the computer that knows how to make the most minute adjustments at the right time preventing the entire system from shutting down.

All that I say to you is for deeper thought. It is for those who are ready to awaken and are allowing reality to become an active part of their lives.

In reality, you will always be what you are, and that is Love. If you will just be Love, loving yourself first that you might love others, this is the most important message I can give you or you can give the world. I give you my Love.

- *Suggested Meditation* -
Expanding Your Consciousness
Page 139

CHAPTER 5

Recognizing Truth—Living In Joy And The Power Of Reality

Seek the reality of truth and Love,
and it will find you.

This is Jesus, and I wish to say *everything I say to you is given in Love.* There are many teachers on your planet at this time, and there are many teachers in the nonphysical realm that are surrounding your planet. A tremendous amount of information is being given to you from both sources.

I say to you, *as you receive this information, be certain it comes from a universal consciousness of Love.* If the information is not given from Love, it is given from ego. When I speak of ego, I am speaking of your belief that you are separate from your Creator. This belief has created a fear, causing a need to find safety within your fear. The belief and the fear are illusions, for there is no basis in reality for this belief. When information is given by the ego, it can always be known, for scattered through the truth, like small grains of sand, will be elements of fear.

There are many untrue beliefs that have developed in your universe and many universes beyond. In other universes, the term ego may not be used, but the belief system is entrapped by an illusion. When a thought is shared from illusion, it cannot be reality. You are rather receiving a shadow of the truth. When truth is not given, your belief in illusion is being enhanced.

It is important on your planet at this time for you to begin to express from truth. Now, how can you do this if you do not know what truth is? Truth is not just new and interesting information. It is not stored records. It is not even events of what you perceive to be your future. Truth is reality. Know that to interchange the words reality and truth, is what is.

This is the God-essence. This is the purity of creation. For you to recognize the illusion in others' communications, you must first know the difference between truth and illusion.

All illusion is built upon a shadow of truth. Therefore, the information of illusion can be factual but not actual.

Please think about this. It can be a fact that Sue went to see Tom today. You know it. You saw Sue get in the car. When you drove by Tom's house, Sue's car was there. They were on the porch. You saw both people. Fact. Your eyes saw it. You know it.

Actually the reality of Sue may not have even been on this planet. Sue may have been in a fatal accident on her way to Tom's. However, your belief and the illusion of your belief supported what you thought was fact. Because you saw someone on the porch and an automobile similar to Sue's, it supported your illusion of fact, and you truly believed what "your eyes saw." The illusion that your mind creates saw the fact of that illusion. Actual could have been much different.

Let us use the example of John the actor. John the actor is playing Hamlet, and he is every bit expressing Hamlet in the illusion of the play. As you view him, the fact is you see the play, and he plays the part of Hamlet. This is fact. Actually, he is John, a much different personality and individual soul, even though the factual information supported him to be Hamlet. If you were not experienced at attending the drama of the theater, you would believe John to be Hamlet. All your senses say this is factual, but indeed it is not actual. Presently, your analytical mind understands the illusion—which is factual—of your creations but does not have the ability to separate illusion from the reality which is actual.

You cannot trust facts to be actual. Had you not been trained to know this was a play and the setting supported what you saw, you might think this was actual, as you saw the event to be.

You drive by a friend's house and that friend is having a tremendous confrontation in the front yard. You see it. Your friend is arguing and screaming at another person. Both individuals begin hitting each other, and you know what you see. You believe your friends are angry at each other. What if they were rehearsing for a play? You do not truly know which scenario is actual or factual.

Factual is not actual. It's important for you to be able to make this distinction because as you sort through the events that are going to transpire on your planet, you are going to see a great amount of fact that is not reality. If you do not know how to sort out the truth, you are going to be deceived, and you are going to choose to play a part in the play, which, after a time, becomes your truth. You have forgotten how to express the richness of your true creativity.

By forgetting how to express the richness of your true creativity, you are no longer able to separate illusion from reality. You have become ensnared in what seems to be real versus the reality of what truly is.

You are caught in the game of life. Am I saying to you, do not play? No; I am not saying that to you. You chose to be on the planet, and you are a part of the play. It reflects the actual reality of who you are at all levels of consciousness and in all universes. How are you playing the game? That is what is important. Are you playing your role with love or are you unhappy and unfulfilled in your life? Are you excited about life? Can you not wait to wake up in the morning to begin a new day?

If you are excited about life and cannot wait to begin a new day each morning, you are reflecting what is truly actual about how you are expressing your soul. When you have this realization, it is a wonderful teaching tool to help you to refine and beautify what you want the totality of your individual soul to be. If you didn't have the playground called planet Earth, it might be more difficult for you to recognize the totality of your soul. Remember your individual soul expresses in many levels of consciousness and other dimensions. Earthly physical reflects this totality. Your third-dimensional being on Earth has the ability of great awareness and freewill to recognize and change the illusion to reality.

Now, of course, beyond the drama of the play is the truth of who you are. The truth of who you are will always be the true reality. Your soul experience on Earth depends upon how much you are allowing the reality to express through this experience and reflect into the illusion of present day life on Earth.

Each step of the way has a wonderful, divine purpose. You cannot ignore the illusion. It is, however, important to know the difference between the illusion and reality, the difference between fear and Love. When you begin expressing in total reality, illusion is no longer illusion. Illusion is transformed into reality. It no longer is reflecting reality; it is reality in expression. Humanity is presently taking these steps of awakening.

Yet, there are many souls who are living in the illusion believing they are complete with the illusion they have created. They have no desire to awaken to the reality of who they truly are because they are comfortable with the control of the ego. These souls understand manipulation; it makes them feel powerful. Because their ego is empowered, they believe they are powerful. They believe that if they move out of the illusion of control and manipulation, they will have no power. Therefore, these souls expend a great deal of effort keeping the illusion alive.

If you are playing the game of control or manipulation, you are giving power to this illusion. You can be on that wheel for eons of time, if that is the path your soul chooses. As long as you allow another to control what you are doing or when you feel the only way for you to be safe is to manipulate those around you, no matter how large or small either of these circumstances may seem to be, you will never be free from the illusion. You will never express the true power of your reality.

As humanity, you seem to find it very difficult to feel safe in your physical existence without control and manipulation. You do not like to think you are controlling, and you do not like to think you are manipulating, but I would challenge you to choose any day of your life you either wish to reflect upon or one in which you choose that morning to conduct a honest search for the existence of these two ego tools in your life. If, indeed, you are totally free of one or both of these, you are truly well along the path of remembrance. Place a very bright star in the heavens of your soul's journey.

If you discover you are caught in the trap of ego control and manipulation, you now have awakened within your soul a great and powerful awareness. This is a wonderful place to begin.

You can only be free of these ego tools when you no longer are entrapped by your judgments. When you judge, you are choosing to place a value system upon a person or circumstance. As long as you have judgments, you will feel the need to manipulate and control or to be manipulated and/or controlled. Without judgment, you are free to love both yourself and others. Judgment is a bondage of control.

Living In Truth

To live in truth, you must recognize truth. To recognize truth, you must recognize who you are.

You must believe the essence of your being is the essence of your Creator and that you are perfect in every way. Every truth of the universe that is, is in the now moment. It is all within your soul. You find this truth through the path of your Spirit, the Spirit of God within you. This truth can always be accessed by you; therefore, all truth is within your ability to know.

The Creator did not create you and then withhold from you the access to being all that you can be.

Your stumbling block lies in finding the way through your mental perceptions of limitation and fear and your belief that illusion is reality.

Do you know what I wish could be done for humanity? I wish for one short period of time every activity would stop on your planet, every modern invention would become inoperable, and humanity would have nothing to do but be in the quietness and the stillness of your beautiful planet. I wish during that time you would examine yourself, relate to yourself, remember yourself. In so doing, it would be like a 10,000 year reflection by the mass consciousness upon your experience in the illusion.

You can create a time of reflection if you choose. You can find that quiet, 24-hours, days or weeks to be totally alone, hopefully awakening to all the creations of your illusions that you might begin to examine your creations and discover who you are.

You often touch into this awareness during your quiet time of meditation when you are blanking out all of the illusion, and you are coming directly into the truth of your being. The truth of your being will never fail you. It will always guide you and lead you in a straight upward spiral. You are moving in a circle only because you choose the path of illusion rather than journeying upward in a spiral listening to the truth of who you are.

Truth is. You are. God is. God is Love. You are Love. Truth is Love. You can live your existence on Earth in all the factual information you desire. You can run through the brilliantly designed maze that humanity has designed, calling it truth.

What do I mean by the maze? I mean all the things you are taught you must do and be to have a safe and happy life. The maze is a design of illusion; it is composed of rules. This illusion has become comfortable for you. You are comfortable with people telling you what to do, and you are comfortable with the direction rules provide. Following a known path is familiar and comfortable. There are those souls who will gladly construct for you a maze of illusion to follow. They will provide sign posts or they, themselves, will guide you through this wonderfully constructed maze of illusion, and it feels comfortable. The walls are gold, the floors are colorful, the maze is rich with illusion; it appears to be so real.

If you choose to live in illusion, it is probably the best way to live in illusion. But, I'm saying to you, *it is not going to work on this planet with the transformation taking place because the maze will not hold.* It is not secure. You've become so accustomed to running through this maze of illusion that you are not going to recognize the corrosion process of the maze as it begins. The maze becomes tighter and more difficult to move through. Finally, it comes to a dead end. You have no place to go. There are no new rules. Rules no longer are a tool for conduct on your planet.

If you continue to choose the illusion of fear, you will become a part of all that is not real. I desire the entire world to hear this message. The age draws near when you must live in the reality of truth.

The illusion is beginning to crumble,
confusion will reign, and you will be unable
to understand why this is happening
because you followed the rules of illusion.

You did all the things you were told. You were good, kind and compassionate. You performed the rituals and the ceremonies. You joined the organizations and you attended the meetings. You did whatever you've been told you must do to find your salvation of truth on the planet.

How can you find truth on a planet that is not truth? When all of your planet is an illusion, how can you find truth when the truth you believe is itself created by illusion? You must go within yourself. You must listen to your soul and Spirit.

What I say to you is only to awaken you to all that you are. I say to you, *I came to help you recognize all that you are. You are no different from me. It is only that you do not know this truth because you are trapped in all you have come to believe.* It's a trap of illusion. You played your part in the game. You played it lifetime after lifetime. The illusion of the game has become your truth. You ask, "What do you mean when you say this isn't reality?"

If John enacts the role of Hamlet every day, he may begin to believe he is Hamlet. But, he is not. He's still John. Just because his mind has convinced him he is Hamlet doesn't change the fact of who he is. You must recognize the truth before you can live in the truth.

When you choose to express from pure Love which is the truth of reality, you are no longer running through a maze. You are being. You are expressing through the power of Love. You no longer need nor are in bondage to the maze of your illusion. Living a rich, abundant life of joy and prosperity occurs through the reality of Love.

Now may I answer any questions you may have regarding what has been said? It is of the utmost importance at this time that you begin to recognize truth.

Q: What is truth for us?

When you recognize reality, you recognize truth. To recognize reality, place it beside illusion. Then you will know the difference. Truth is an inner knowing separating illusion from reality. It's a process. It's a process because you are clearing lifetimes of perceptions and belief in illusion.

As you begin to place truth beside illusion, there is a very subtle knowing within you that begins to recognize, "This is illusion. This is truth."

You've had glimpses of this knowing. There have been times in the depth of your being you've known what is truth and what is illusion. It may only have been a glimpse, and you may not have realized this was what was taking place. You will become aware of this knowing as it grows. To know you know, is revelation. This knowing does not come from learning or an outside informational source. Think of a time you knew something to be truth, you just "knew it" and no matter the illusion presented to you, your knowing was not shaken. This is living in the reality of actual, not factual.

The important principle is to move into the realm of truth, into reality, leaving the fear of illusion. As you see glimpses, you will choose to live in this reality of Love. I desire for you to see the illusion for what it is. The more you desire to know truth, the more you will receive this revelation. Those souls who have a near-death experience find life is never the same. This is because they caught a glimpse of reality free from the illusion. That is why life is never the same. They "know" there is a reality of Love. It does not mean they will always live in that reality, but they caught a glimpse of the possibility. They experienced the truth of Love.

The truth of reality is very powerful because it is real, because it is what is. It doesn't mean you are going to leave the illusion of your world. Rather the illusion becomes reality. You are still going to live on this planet. If you have the beautiful realization of truth and reality and you leave the planet, what have you done for humanity? How have you helped others to recognize the illusion?

You only need to recognize illusion. You must live in the reality of truth while recognizing the illusion around you. When you reach this awakening, you shift the illusion. The illusion of fear is transformed and Love becomes your reality. This is the New Heaven and New Earth. You then live in the beautiful reality of truth. Your soul is housed in your physical body with your own personal creations on the planet. Made perfect, physical existence is beautiful.

It is only your belief you are separate and can be destroyed that creates the illusion of fear. If, indeed, you were actually separate from your spiritual essence, your existence would not be possible. Therefore, know your belief of separation from your spiritual essence is only an illusion.

You have become so entrapped by this illusion that the illusion has become your reality. You do not know what truth and reality are any longer. You no longer remember your reality for it has been replaced by illusion.

Q: When you are going within to find this truth, is there some kind of signal, something we can focus on, to know it is truth and not further illusion?

Seek the truth, and it will find you.

The key is setting your intent and trusting in who you truly are. Your intent to find reality will open the door. As you seek, you may say along the way this is different; this must be truth. It may only be another layer of illusion that you continue peeling and peeling and peeling, until you finally connect to the purity, the reality of creation. You will know without a question or doubt when it is truth. A deep, inner knowing of revelation will guide you.

When you know truth, you will know unconditional love. Perhaps I should stop here and define unconditional love. It is not the emotion of love. Unconditional love is honoring and respecting all creations, tangible and intangible because they exist. It is truly the golden rule of the oneness of all life. You do not worry about unknown dangers when you love unconditionally. When you love unconditionally, you create from the reality of Love and interact in harmony with all life. When you create from fear and illusion, you are often a perceived threat to the illusion of others. When you live and create from the reality of Love, you are no longer subject to the illusion. You have no fear of others nor they of you.

The reason you do not love unconditionally is because you think illusion is real, and, therefore, harm will come to you if you love unconditionally. When you love unconditionally, you transform the illusion.

You presently expend much energy protecting yourself from the illusion that isn't even real. When you love unconditionally, there is no harm possible because there is no harm in reality.

The more you are expressing from unconditional love, the more you are living in reality. The more you realize that the creations of illusion are unimportant to you, the more you are living in reality. Let me explain what I mean by, the more the illusion is unimportant. Let us examine this concept by looking at your surroundings, the positions that you hold, the respect from others that you feel you need, for all of this is the importance of the illusion. To feel you need the respect or the love of your brother or sister is again the ego illusion. You feel these needs because the validation of others confirms that illusion is reality. The more these things are unimportant to you, the less you are empowering the illusion. You are no longer in need of ego validation. Reality is complete within itself.

The more the illusion is unimportant, the more you are living in reality. You begin to have a deep, inner peace that grows. You become aware of the beauty of all life, the expansiveness of creation. When you empower the illusion, you imprison yourself. You are struggling with minute unimportant details, and you are making them the most important things in your life.

Let go. When you begin to replace the illusion with reality, all is so much brighter, more beautiful and enjoyable. You no longer go through the frustration of creating from your ego. Illusion will create illusion. Reality is. Your creative ability flows. You no longer work at creating your good. It's just there. It is.

It takes faith to let go of what you believe to be real. It takes trust because you now trust the illusion. Illusion is familiar to you. It works for you. You may wonder, "How do I learn to trust what you call reality when I do not even know how to find this reality?" It is not easy to do when you are living from the perceptions of your ego and your mind. However, when you choose to remember who you are, you place in motion the deep, inner knowing of your soul. It is subtle.

*Go within, quiet the arguments of the mind and listen to your Spirit. It will become more and more real to you each day. Life will flow. Joy fills your days; you glow with the radiance of true expression. That is when you begin to express and live from your **real** power.*

When you express in the reality of All That Is, all of the illusion is meaningless. Whatever you need is created without control or manipulation. You no longer desire to live in the illusion because freedom is experienced when expressing in the beauty of reality. You are no longer trapped and held in bondage inside the maze of illusion that has been created on the planet.

How do you create from the power of reality? You create from the power of reality by being reality; being what you are, Love. Do not allow another to entrap you in their belief that illusion is truth. Do not get caught into their games. If they choose to play in the illusion of creation, so be it.

Now is the time to move into truth, to live in reality. I ask you to remember the oneness of life thereby freeing your planet of the illusion of separateness. I ask you to awaken into the reality that you are, in order to once again experience the beauty of your world. Free yourself from the self-imposed imprisonment of illusion and humanity. Choose to lay down the tools of war, anger, pollution, economic controls, hatred and selfishness. You've created all these structures thinking they serve you somehow and believing these tools of illusion give you power.

It is of great importance that this message be recognized as vital. The time is now. The message of Love and reality must be spread. Begin living your life from the reality of Love. Begin recognizing the illusion you've created, understanding it has no purpose. It isn't even real. Move into the truth of who you are.

I give to you unconditional love. I touch the very depth of your soul to give you the realization of what I am saying. You must choose the reality of Love and truth to free yourself from the entrapment of illusion.

Q: Many of us have been trying to do this over a period of time, yet there seem to be many blocks that make it seem difficult and not as easy as dropping illusion and moving into reality. Can you address the forces that keep that from happening? Is it resistance? Is it a fear of letting go of what seems comfortable?

It's all of those, but remember it is still all a part of the illusion that has been created. To you the illusion is very real. When you say, "I'm going to move into reality," even when you make a mental commitment to move into reality, you do not know what reality is, for your mind only knows the illusion. When you do not see immediate success, you either feel you've failed or the reality of which I speak doesn't exist. You may then decide illusion and reality are all the same. You may say, "I tried and it didn't work for me."

Remember you've taken eons of time to build the many layers of illusion. It is your well-constructed defense system for you feel you are not safe. Do not expect to move through those well-structured layers without resistance from your ego. It's not going to happen because there are too many solid walls, too many well-placed layers. But, I can promise you this, make the commitment to give the time, be willing and set your intent to live in reality and life will become easier with greater clarity of vision. The knowing of your inner truth will begin to expand into your conscious mind. Choose to express and live from this truth and reality. By so doing, your life will begin to change.

Ask for help. How often do you forget to ask for the help? I will help you. The angels will help you. We can help you move the layers. Think of it as your hands pushing against the wall of illusion with ten more hands behind your hands. The wall will begin to crumble much faster when you remember to ask for our help. However, we cannot move the wall at all until you begin to push it aside because it is your creation. It is your illusion. You have a freewill right to keep the illusion intact.

Think of your creations of illusion as a beautiful temple you've constructed having built it over millions of years, a brick at a time, a gold layer at a time. It is ornate, unique, and it is beautiful. Now you ask, "You want me to destroy my eons of creations?" Know you are not really destroying anything. You are identifying the illusion of the creation versus the reality.

I have said to you when you create, your creation exists forever. The illusion exists as illusion and must continually be empowered and validated to serve you. You need to be able to identify the illusion from the reality. It is now time to express the reality of all that you are. Many of your creations of illusion have become self-destructive. If you continue creating in that vein, the creations are going to tumble, and you will not have the illusion.

You say, "Well, not having illusion would be pretty wonderful." Well, no it truly wouldn't because again illusion is what you believe to be your reality. The illusion is like a picture on a canvas. The picture is a facsimile of the object or person it represents. But if you have never seen the three-dimensional object, the two-dimensional picture on canvas has the capability of expressing the object at a lesser vibration. Illusion is a mere reflection of the reality of your soul. It is important that you not destroy the illusion, but rather recognize and bring forth the reality within the illusion. Physical is important even though it presently exists encased in total illusion. Recognize the illusion and live in reality.

As you begin to express your reality, you are going to refine and perfect the illusion through transformation. Nothing is destroyed; it is transformed. How can you transform illusion? By returning to the unconditional, nonjudgmental reality of Love. This is the key.

Q: What is the difference between happiness and joy?

What you see as an expression of joy comes from the reality of Love. If you see an emotion expressed, it may be a moment of happiness, but it often lacks depth. Happiness can be for only a fleeting moment. It can be stolen by the next words that are spoken. It depends on external motivation.

The more the reality of the Love that you are expresses through your emotions, the more you know joy. This is the true expression of reality, and it is the laugh that is contagious. It is the expression of joy that touches into your soul. Joy doesn't mean you are happy because everything is going wonderfully well in your life. The joy in your heart does not depend on circumstances. You may have just gone through a most challenging situation, but you still feel the joy deep within your soul.

Joy is not emotion. It is an expression of the reality of the existence of Love. Happiness is a momentary effect of illusion in the physical. Joy from deep within your soul is a state of being and has nothing to do with outer circumstances.

Joy does not live within fear.

So often in your religious structure, because of the doctrine of unworthiness, shame, guilt, and fear, the belief in the illusion is strengthened. The effect is you feel more fear; you strengthen the belief that you are separate from your Creator. Still searching for the joy, you follow the rules wondering what is missing, why you do not have a deep joy in your heart.

However, I must say, there are those moments in your structured religious beliefs you touch the truth of reality. Reality will always bring joy so you experience glimpses of joy. Religion, therefore, has served you as a vehicle, a maze, a tool in which to search for the reality of who you truly are.

At this time, I give you my blessings and my Love. I do love you so very much, and know I am with you always.

- Suggested Meditation -
The Light Of Love
Page 135

CHAPTER 6

Rediscovering The Brilliant Soul
That You Are

*Let the divinity in each cell of your body rise like
the sun—illuminating the darkness of illusion
with the brilliance of love to show you
the reality of your being.*

This is Jesus, and I bring to you the greetings and the Love of the Creator. I give you this message to awaken the power that lies within your soul. All that has been said has been for the purpose of bringing to you the awareness of the essence of who you are. The goal is to give you a mental awareness of truths that are already within your own being. You might then begin to process these truths within your own consciousness recognizing them as they surface from your soul and Spirit.

I say to you, *if you desire to live fully all that you are and in the power of the moment, separate the illusion from the reality.* As you separate the illusion from the reality, you move from plodding through the illusion into the freedom of spiritual awareness. In the reality, you become aware of the purity of all existence.

The illusion is a reflection, seen through a glass darkly, of the reality. It is distorted. Specks appear on the glass, fingerprints mar its surface and the reflection is not as pristine and beautiful as the true reality of truth. You ask,

67

"Can you not just wipe the glass clean, remove the specks and see the truth?" No, it is still only the reflection that is called illusion. You must move into the reality to recognize truth.

I now speak to you regarding the emotion of love and the reality of Love. I have spoken to you so often of the word Love. Love is All That Is. Love is truth. God is Love. You are Love. Yet, I know you do not fully understand my meaning when I say "Love." I recognize your understanding of love is through the illusion of your creations, the interactions on the physical level of emotions that you believe must be love. It makes you feel good. The emotion of love heightens your awareness of the beauty around you, and you are happy. You feel alive. This must be love. But, it isn't. It's an aspect of your emotional body.

Love is everything that is. Everything exists as it is, in its completeness. Love is the totality of all creation because creation is the expression of the Creator, and the Creator is Love. This is the reality of Love. It is all that is, and it is you. I would like to substitute another word, but there is no other word to give you because your emotion of love is the closest mental concept you have of the beauty of truth. When I say Love, I would like for you to cleanse your mind of your definition of the word and listen as though this were a brand-new word.

I will call it Divine Love. Let that be removed one step from the love, the deepest love you have ever known or felt. You are, must be and can be no other than Divine Love. Divine Love is All That Is, and it is perfect. Therefore, everything that exists is perfect. Everything that exists is reality. Reality is experienced through the imperfect perception of illusion. Reality is complete perfection, total knowing of All That Is, unlimited awareness.

You feel if you are widely traveled, highly educated and

very intelligent, you are a very aware being. The standard you set is your present limited awareness on this planet. Consider the three-month old baby that plays with the toys in its crib. The baby develops a whole new world of awareness. The small fingers touch a solid object; the baby's mind processes it. This is certainly a larger physical world than the infant has known in the early days of its infancy. The child is feeling very grown up at three months old; did you know that? This soul is rediscovering the physical world.

You look at a three-month old child, and you are very happy as he or she explores each new discovery because this tells you the child is developing in all the normal capacities. You believe, however, this is not all the child will ever know. Picture yourself as the three-month old child. Being given every toy that fits into your playpen, you've explored and played with each one of them believing you know and understand your playpen environment. You have learned if you push a certain button a bell will ring, and if you pull on the ring beside the green color, the clown's head will go around. Having learned how to live in your environment, you understand life very well as you believe it to be in your playpen.

Not only do you believe you know your way around your world better than many of the other babies, you may also believe you have learned more. You believe you've done a good job. Indeed, in your belief that illusion is reality, you have become extraordinary beings. It's a game you play. Someone built the toys and that someone was you. You have refined and perfected the toys in your playpen while the mind has grown sharper processing data more quickly. You, as humanity, now have a wonderful awareness of your entire planet—the awareness of your playground has expanded.

It was not very long ago, not very long ago at all, that

most of humanity had no such awareness of the entire planet Earth. You knew only of your own special territory, the other souls much like your own who lived there and the limited creations with which you interacted. How quickly your mental processes have moved from not only the awareness of your own little playground called Earth but expanded into the universe. You are now ready to take the step of recognizing reality. In reality you state, "I stand back from it all, and I realize I am not the illusion of fear and pain. I am pure God energy. Love energy."

As you move into reality, you begin to recognize you have a beautiful playground, the planet Earth. You will take care of it because it enriches all you have created. The planet is not the reality of who you are, but it is an enrichment to all your creations.

Much of your creation is physical and your physical needs the physical planet Earth. If you choose not to take care of your planet, you believe it will not support your physical life form. It is not your survival as a soul that is in question; it is your physical creations that have need of a physical Earth. Your soul is not physical and shall exist forever as your unique, individual expression of God.

When I see humanity so entrapped in all of the illusion of fear, I wish it were within my power to reveal to you your pure vibrational forms, even for one brief moment.

If two souls could, for even a moment, relate to one another on this planet in your purest forms—the two of you relating only as light energy, Love energy, the essence of your beings— you would never ever become upset, angry or disturbed by that soul again.

All disharmony would melt into the nothingness from which it came.

The New Cycle of Experience

What you fear is illusion. Illusion isn't worth the effort you give to it. Your emotions distort and create even more layers of illusion. Why is it now important to recognize this illusion? After all, you are living on the planet, you are physical, it all seems so real to you, so why is it important to separate illusion from reality? It is important because you are entering a new cycle of experience by your soul. The illusion will no longer work for you.

Those who do not heal the entrapment of their illusion are going to remain trapped by the illusion. When they are trapped in the illusion and the illusion no longer works, it will create chaos, for those souls have only a shallow awareness of reality. Awaken now, for your soul feels an urgency to awaken to reality. You will lead the way to a restored humanity, a fully-awakened consciousness of Divine Love.

What has your illusion done for you? The belief in the illusion of separation from your Creator has caused you to turn to the illusion to keep you safe. Almost all your effort is expended into creating more illusion. Little energy is placed on remembering the reality.

Reality has become buried deeper and deeper and deeper until it is only a shadow in your memory. The layers of illusion can stretch so far, and illusion will become nonexistent because it isn't real. Your layers are stretching to the limits. If humanity were to choose to continue in the illusion, the illusion would become so real to you even though it is nonexistent, your conscious mind would be lost to the awareness of reality forever.

Let the divinity in each cell of your body rise like the

sun—illuminating the darkness of illusion with the brilliance of Love to show you the reality of your being.

As an expression of the Creator, the reality of Love and truth exists within your Spirit always.

God does not judge nor proclaim your destiny. The path of your soul is always your freewill choice. This is why your soul begins to search becoming aware something is lacking in your creative expression on the planet. You begin to question the reality of the illusion. Because there is a vast spectrum of individual soul awareness, there may be one who says, "I truly want to know the reality of my own being" while another is working desperately to improve the illusion.

Therefore, those who are searching to know the reality of Love are the salvation for those who are blindly creating the illusion. Will you snatch them from their illusion? No, of course not. That is for them to do. However, the awareness you are Love allows the beauty of your creative expression of all that you are to flow, healing your world. Living in the reality that you are Love helps to awaken the reality of Love in every person your energy touches.

Love is the hope of those souls not yet beginning to awaken. When the mass consciousness reaches a critical mass, all souls begin to search for the truth of Love. All will awaken, for all life is one.

My friends, I must tell you, you cannot free yourself from the illusion completely until the illusion is no longer. You can choose to be in the now reality, but you cannot free yourself completely from the illusion until it no longer exists. Now, I know someone is thinking, "Yes, I can." You may transcend this Earth this very moment, but the Love of who you are would not let you walk away from your brothers and your sisters and leave them entrapped. That, my friends, means you are not free.

When you are truly awake and aware, your love would never allow you to forget others, for you know they are you. You know all life is one. The recognition of the worth of the soul is so great, and your love is so profound, you would not walk away as long as there is one soul who is not free of the illusion.

I want to stop and ask if you have any questions.

Q: You said that we wouldn't be free of the illusion until all were free of the illusion, so is our goal to become aware of the illusion if we cannot be free of the illusion?

Consciously knowing reality makes you extremely aware of illusion. However, you are not free because you would not choose to be unaware of the illusion as long as any soul is entrapped. Realize you are all one and there is a part of you still entrapped. Until every soul is free, all are not free.

Q: When we're free of illusion, does that mean the illusion will no longer exist, or will we be able to see the difference?

It means you are free to continue creating. Creations of reality contain no fear and exist in complete harmony with all other creations. That is the difference. All creations respect and honor all other creations for they are without the need to defend their existence. Creations of reality know their completeness and exist in the totality of their Creator.

You will always be creating, and you will always be creating from freewill. It was from freewill and reality that you created illusion. As you return to the awareness of your reality, think of the wonderful creations you may next bring into existence.

Q: You say we're living from freewill, and I think we accept that, yet the highest form of freewill is to give God's will precedence in our lives. Does this mean we actually turn over our lives to God and His will be done, or does it mean we live in the essence of love at all times which is God's will for all of us?

What is God's will? God's will is that you express your completeness of Love reality in total conscious awareness. When you are so buried in the illusion, how is this possible? As you remember you are God expressing in the physical, you live from the Spirit, the God-essence within you. You allow your Spirit to guide your soul which is your own individual expression of God. This awareness penetrates the frightened ego sending new messages of reality to the conscious mind.

You begin with surrender. It is the surrender of your conscious, analytical mind to your soul and your soul to your Spirit. You do this by making an active choice. You choose. Freewill allows you to choose each moment of your existence. This choice is to surrender and be willing to walk in the truth that you know is yours. Ask that this truth be enhanced; seek to be shown a deeper and deeper understanding of reality.

As you recognize truth, you also realize truth is Love.

You are then living your life from the reality of Love, you are walking in the truth that is Love.

If you think about this, some of the most loving, kind people you may know do not even have an awareness of these qualities. They are not trying to be loving and kind and good. That is who they are. They walk daily in a quiet harmony with life because they are not quite as entrapped in the illusion. Are they better than you? Are they smarter? Are they more holy? No. They're just not quite as entrapped.

When you are entrapped in illusion, you become entrapped in your perceived needs. Your perception of these needs and how to obtain them create pressure. The pressure creates stress, and the stress creates physical, mental and emotional problems. Your energy is now placed in a survival mode which is the entrapment of illusion. Illusion demands you work very hard to continue creating more illusion.

You must make a conscious choice to return to the reality of who you are, to reclaim the true power of the God-self within.

Amazingly enough, as you seek the reality of truth and Love it seeks you.

You find your desires change. Your needs lessen. Your entire life begins to change. You draw to you the people, books and circumstances that will help you rediscover who you are.

Notice the person that seems unassuming, who smiles from the joy within his or her heart. That person is awakening to inner truth. That person is kind, compassionate, understanding without a need to control or manipulate others. I am not saying to you to deny yourself all the wonders of your planet. I am saying, *do not be entrapped by them.*

Your question, I believe, was concerning God's will. The will of the Creator is Love because it is All That Is, only Love. It is not the emotion of love, it is the Love that is God in expression.

When you live in the reality of Love, your whole being, your whole perspective on life changes. Those around you see you differently. The way of the ego is the perception of safety by the need to control and manipulate to get through life. It is so shallow compared to walking in the power of your own reality. Ego power is one of the games of illusion. Ego power enhances illusion and causes it to continue. It creates much pain. Love heals and frees the soul.

Q: Does illusion only apply while on planet Earth?

No, it doesn't just apply to life on the planet Earth, but because of your physical existence on planet Earth, it is here you have created the greatest layers of illusion. You are not free from the illusion when you leave this planet. The illusion is still very powerful and often draws you back to Earth sooner than you are ready because the physical is a solid reflection of illusion. This is what your planet has become, a reflection of the illusion, a reflection of illusion so real to you that it masks who you are and all that you are.

Q: How do we find out exactly what our reality is?

My friend, if I could give you a short discourse, the world would not be where it is. It's a process of awakening to awareness.

But, if you are not aware that illusion exists, you do not know to begin to seek reality. Think of ten people you know and say to them "This world is an illusion." They most likely are not going to agree with you. For them it is reality. They say, "How can it be an illusion? I see. I touch. I feel. I smell. I experience all these senses. My emotions are real. I feel them. They're very real." These people do not understand the concept of illusion. If you understand the concept of illusion, you are on your path to reality.

As you travel your path of awakening, two guidelines to follow are: how much are you letting go of the perception of safety found in the illusion, and how unconditionally do you choose to love?

Those are two very important guidelines you can set for yourself to know you are moving out of the illusion into reality.

Now, I want to clarify what has been said so there is no misunderstanding. Healing illusion doesn't mean if you choose to drive the most expensive car on this planet it is wrong because it is not wrong. If you live in the biggest house on the tallest hill, so be it. The illusion is to be entrapped by these things, and there is a vast difference. Do you NEED them for the fulfillment of your life?

Do you enjoy your car, your home, etc. because you are

in the physical and these bring physical enjoyment, or are they important to you because you need them to make you feel important, good, worthwhile or safe? For most of humanity, the material possessions of life give them a sense of value, of who they are, of their worth to society. This is a false sense of identity and is the entrapment in illusion. Experience the joy in all of your journey on this planet. You have created many toys, enjoy them, but do not become entrapped by these, your creations.

Physical is beautiful. You are here. Enjoy it. PLAY, have a good time in the physical. Indeed, it is a powerful way to express your creative power. There is nothing wrong with physical existence. I do not want to leave you with that impression. In fact, the more you can play in the physical without needing any of it, the more you become aware of reality. The more important the illusion of your physical is to you, the more you are going to work very hard at being a part of the illusion and the more you are entrapped by it.

I touch into your soul that your soul might touch the mind and that it might open a clearer path back to your Spirit, back to you, the beautiful, pure, wonderful Love that you are, and I give you my Love and my blessings.

- Suggested Meditation -
The Healing Power Of A Rose Petal
Page 147

CHAPTER 7

The Creative Power Within You

As you continuously create from your highest awareness of existence, you are well on your path to perfect Love, joy, peace and harmony, for that is giving of your spiritual self in the creative process.

This is Jesus, and I come to you from the Love of the Father. I thought it might be helpful to explain when I say to you, *I come from the Love of the Father*, what is meant by this term. The term simply means giving of your higher nature, giving of self in a selfless way in the creative process with nonjudgment of your creation knowing you empower your creation as Creator to continue the creation process. This is the God principle. Father brings forth the seed of life. The life must be nurtured, it must expand and it must grow. That is why it has the power of creation.

What is it I convey when I say, *I come to you from the Love of the Father?* When I speak of the word Love, I speak of a word that appeals to your emotions and your mental capacities, a word that encompasses what you believe to be safety and a feeling of peace, harmony and happiness. This is what you convey in your word love. When I speak of Love, I am not speaking of your feeling of emotions.

The Love of the Father is a creative love that continues to always expand, co-creating, giving of itself in the creative process. So when I say to you, *I come from the Love of the Father, I am saying I come from the co-creative principle of expansion that is always giving of self in the continuing creative process.*

How is it one co-creates, giving of self in the creative process? As you continuously create from your highest awareness of existence, you will find you are well on your path to perfect Love, joy, peace and harmony, for that is giving of your spiritual self in the creative process.

Know with a certainty, creations can never be separated from their creator. You, as creator, are co-creator with God, God being the eternal principle of all existence, of All That Is. You being a co-creator with that principle are always expanding self as your creations become a part of you. Your creations become creator and continue to create and create.

In the first thought sent forth, the very seed that would continue existence was planted. Creation would have little value if it were not endowed with the principle of creation so life might expand its own creative process.

You as an expression of creative principle endow your creations with the ability to create as you were so endowed.

That is why when you have a thought, as co-creator with God, it is a creation that becomes a creator. This is the ever-expanding principle of creating from self, of always giving of self.

Every creation has equal value. You, as one creative stream, are as important as all other creations that exists, and you are equal to every creation that exists. You are a part of every creation. Understand the concept you are All That Is; All That Is resides within you. The planets are not "out there"; they are within you and exist as projections of your creative power.

What you believe to be the reality of your universe is only a reflection of the consciousness of humanity. You enjoy interacting with the reflection from the vibrations of your creative energies. The purpose of creative process is to enjoy the creations, enjoying the reflection of what you have created within yourself. If you have no perception of pain, fear, good or bad, you are free to enjoy every creation you have created.

Transformation is finding beauty in all creations, being one with your creations, loving and nurturing your creations because they are the beautiful effects of the creative process.

When you do this, you will dissipate anything that is painful, fearful or damaging to society.

Your Creations Create

Your single act of creation would have little effect if that creation did not become creator. It would eventually become disassembled into creations stronger than itself, the created, much as you might think of your physical body returning to dust and becoming earth again. The single creation would become disembodied within itself and return to raw creative energy. This is not what happens.

The creation becomes creator and continues to create. This is why you are so trapped by your emotions. If your created emotions did not become creator, you would not become controlled by emotions. A single feeling would not have the power to usurp all you are and take control. The power of emotional creation to become the creator expands very rapidly. Instantaneous expansion is the very nature of your emotional energy. This is why you can fill a whole room with your love and your light instantly. If you had to fill in this tiny molecule and that tiny molecule of space, then it would be a very slow, evolving process. Because the created becomes the creator, there is a very rapid expansion of energy. It multiplies immensely.

Effects Of Judgments On Creative Process

A soul incarnates on this planet and has fought many battles in past lives. This soul was deeply entrenched in war and perhaps killed many men, women and children all in the name and cause of whatever the soul felt was its creative process. Now this soul has come back again for another lifetime. This time, however, the soul cannot find a place to express or experience war as had been done so many times before. There is no realization by the soul that it is still entrenched in the stream of that creative process. To the soul, war is still its creative goal. Maybe this person becomes a mass murderer, one day taking a gun and shooting people randomly without even knowing why he or she is killing people. This soul is still being driven by that stream of creative process of physical violence that may have started many lifetimes ago.

You help to lock these souls into experiences of this na-ture by your judgments which, in turn, hold the energy of that creative process within their souls. They will die, rein-carnate and still be struggling with the vibrations of physical violence. The violent experiences have become a large part of their energy patterns, and these particular souls will still see violence as their creative process. You can remove your judgments from their acts, and you can look into their beauty and somehow know that every other soul who chooses to die at that person's hand did it of the soul's own freewill. The soul that died had an experience it chose. Release your judgments and hold those souls in your love. Love will reach in and transform the pain and the fear of those experiences. That same group of souls may come back the next time and be a tremendous force for peace on your planet.

You cannot heal a creation if you have never experi-enced it. If you have never chosen the path of physical violence, you cannot understand such a creation. You may, however, have created a fear that physical violence threat-ens your safety. You can heal your own fear. When you do this, you replace fear with the reality of Love. The soul who was a mass murderer may become the soul who de-sires peace on Earth enough to dedicate one entire life experience making a profound difference in your world.

If you bind these souls in their acts labeling the acts as evil, it is very difficult for them to rise above a judgment of evil. The souls are then confused and leave the planet con-fused. Arriving in fourth dimension confused, they shower the vibration of confusion there. These souls continually struggle to move higher, looking for their own salvation. Remove your judgments of these souls for in reality you are also judging and imprisoning yourself. You may not have chosen the experience of physical violence, but if there wasn't something inside of you that continually massacres yourself, you would not see it projected as a part of your reality in the outer.

As your soul began your own unique, individual path, so you began your own individual creations. Your creations were and are creators as are you.

All that is created has the power to create.

Your creations become aware of and intermingle with the creations of other souls. At times in the creative process creations collide resulting in conflict. Strife, turmoil, wars and misunderstandings are the result.

Lifetimes Of Creative Process

When you incarnate on your planet in physical form, you bring the remembrances of all your previous creations with you.

You experience life from the remembrances of your creations rather than from the awareness that you are the creator. You give your power to what you yourself have created. The creations become your master.

When you recognize these creations of illusion have only the power of existence you give to them, then they are no longer a threat or limitation in your life. You are then free to interact with your brothers and sisters from the reality of

Love that you are to the reality of Love that they are. All the annoyances and irritations that have created the discord and disharmony between you disappear into the vast pool of nothingness from which they came.

All the discord that takes place on your planet, creating less than a complete harmonious existence, is created from your belief that you are separated from your Creator.

You are not separate from God, but your ego and your emotions tell you that you are. Listening to them, you believe them and accept them as your reality. The fear within you is created by the ego and the emotions. You fear because your very life source is uncertain. You are not sure where to find the needed substance for your existence. You search for a way to reunite with your Creator.

You have created and programmed your emotions to serve the safety needs of the ego. Emotions are the ego's first line of defense to any perceived threat to your survival. Even the emotion you call love on your planet is a limited love. The emotion of love is a mere reflection of the reality of Love.

Open your soul to the freedom of the reality of Love that you are. I say to you, *read these words without filtering them through your previous understandings, without filtering them through the conscious mind and perceptions of your experiences.* Touch your divinity. Bring forth the reality of your soul and begin to walk in your light.

When you choose to give of self from your lower base

nature of fear and disharmony, you are creating fear and disharmony no matter the mask the creation may wear. The creation then becomes the creator. This is how confusion, fear, and discord are promoted in your world.

But you can change your world. You can create harmony, love, joy and peace. BE all that you are. Be the Love that you are and everything else will change.

Q: Can you describe God, how we originated from God and what God expects from us?

To try to describe God as many see God is like saying, "Somewhere in this vast universe or beyond is some type of a being that is all-knowing, all-superior, and in control of all existence." That is not God; God is creative principle. God is not a limited being; neither is God a single energy force expressing itself in some manner.

God is universal, unconditional, nonjudging Love in expression. As I speak to you of God, God is creative principle without shape, form or limitation. God is ever expanding. As you created today, God expanded and changed.

At this very moment, all creations as they continue to create are God. God is not fixed, and God is not a being. Within the very nucleus of all the expansion of creation, there is undefiled power of unlimited, creative process and unlimited freewill. The creative principle creates your world, other worlds, universes, parallel dimensions, life and death. What you may think of as God is that stream of undefiled principle of unlimited freewill with unlimited creative ability. God exists in everything, for that is the essence of the oneness of life.

God has no expectations. Expectations are created by your own mental consciousness. God neither expects nor demands. God does not administer punishment. God is not a God of judgment; God is All That Is—the ever lasting, eternal, creative process. This is the very nature of existence.

If you desire to contemplate God, think of creative process; think of unlimited, creative ability; and think of that creative process as ever expanding. Your consciousness cannot encompass the depth of God. Comprehending the vastness of continual, creative process without end is not possible for you at this time. Your present consciousness does not understand time and space are illusions, without substance and can collapse at a single, simultaneous thought by humanity. You created it all as God in expression, for all are expressing God.

The Path To Peace And Harmony

It is now time for humanity to clearly become aware and accept that all are the creative process. By allowing recognition of yourselves as creative process, you will have a basis for understanding your existence on this planet; otherwise you will have no such basis for understanding.

If you choose to judge your creative process as good or bad, great or small, you will become snarled and encapsulated by your own creations. You are then no longer free to enjoy what you have created. It is not the creations but the creative process you begin to judge. Think about this. You do not necessarily judge a creation because the creation exists. If it had no power within itself to further create, it would have no consequences in your life, and, therefore, it would have no meaning to you of good nor bad. It could not self-perpetuate. Therefore, what it is that truly entraps you in your fear is the creative process. Deep within you know you are that process. If you are the process and the process is capable of such creations, then you truly fear your own self. You do not fear the creations of another although you may project your fear upon another soul's creation—what you truly fear is the power that lies within you. You fear the knowledge that what you create becomes a part of you, the creator.

How do you find inner peace and harmony with your creative process? First, you must remove the judgments of your creations. As long as you have judgments of your creations, you are in fear of the creative process, fearful of who you are and fearful of your own inner power and your spirituality. As you begin to remove the judgments of your creations, you also begin to free your own creative process. Creative process will always create from your present belief. If you are living from your human survival mode, you will create from false survival instincts. If you are following your soul's path, you will create from your soul's path. If you have moved into the awareness that you are Spirit and eternal, then as your creations flow they will touch all that is around you and transform anything that limits or hinders the creative process by the power of your spirituality.

Just by being in your presence those around you will become more aware of their true essence. They may not always understand or even know exactly what to do with this new awareness. They may even be somewhat uncomfortable as they first enter this new awareness of self-creative power, for this awareness can stir a tremendous latent fear buried within their already frightened ego. You have been in fear of what has been created and now you are remembering you are also responsible for those creations. Therefore, you feel very out of control.

As you create from your spirituality, you will find you help those still in fear without saying a word. The vibration that flows from you will create a beautiful energy field to help others to move into their higher awareness. When you are totally willing to surrender your ego to your Spirit, surrendering your entire life, surrendering all your beliefs in what keeps you safe, you become one with your soul's path. As you surrender to your soul's path, you become aware of the connection of soul to Spirit. You become aware that to follow the soul's path the direction must come from Spirit.

What is a soul path? It is the path you have predetermined you desire to experience when you incarnate into the physical. This is always based upon your knowledge and understanding before you reincarnate upon the planet. If, during an incarnation, your consciousness expands giving you clearer understanding of your existence, the soul's path may choose a different course. You may no longer desire or choose the soul path you originally chose. Do not feel you are predestined to a certain destiny.

For instance, a soul's path at birth could be to accumulate a great amount of wealth just for the experience of having wealth. This is neither good nor bad; it was only the choice of experience for that lifetime. Suddenly there is a great spiritual awakening and the soul no longer desires to accumulate wealth but now the greatest desire is to be of service to humanity. Experiencing wealth, not service, was the original intent of the soul's path.

One path is not greater than nor lesser than the other. It is all just expressions of creation. Your soul's path may change what it chooses to experience as your consciousness expands and you awaken spiritually.

The more you awaken spiritually, the more joy you feel. Joy brings a sense of direction and fulfillment into your chosen experience.

Also, if your soul is not achieving your soul's path, there is always the opportunity for the soul to choose to leave the planet. You may choose a different path or leave and come again under different circumstances. When you understand creative process, you honor a soul's choice and realize there is no need to be sad when a soul says, "Wait a minute. I cannot experience what I chose to experience; therefore, I may need to incarnate into a new set of circumstances".

Q: Can you give any spiritual insights or perspectives on the subject of sex?

Sex evolved when you began to express your consciousness in a physical form and yet wanted oneness. It was the closest manner in which you could experience the spirituality of oneness. If the spiritual essence is not a part of your sexual act, then it becomes a very hollow, shallow and meaningless experience. Indeed, physical sex without spirituality can drain the life force from your energy pattern.

You will then find an emotional imbalance which affects not only the emotional body but the mental and physical energy patterns as well. It is most often not understood that this imbalance in your energy is the root cause of many physical, emotional and mental problems. If sex is not spiritual, it is best left alone.

If the sexual act is embodied with the spiritual consciousness and essence of who you are, it will strengthen your physical body and heal your emotions. It will reawaken in you the awareness of the oneness of life.

When you truly feel that awareness, it allows you to unleash the reality of Love within you. This love has the power to heal and transform your fears.

Procreation is a by-product of sex. As separate beings, you needed to create physical houses for your soul and Spirit to live in a physical world. Sex became your vehicle. Prior to physical bodies, you still had a oneness of soul and Spirit, but it wasn't a physical oneness. The moments you touch into physical oneness in a spiritual sense are the moments you come the closest to experiencing what oneness of all life truly is.

Q: God is unlimited and I suspect could have just as easily created and maintained a world without pain and fear. Is there some knowledge to be gained from pain and fear as well as love? Do we need to experience the full spectrum of emotions in order to appreciate unconditional love?

I would like to gather you as children, sit you down and say to you, *look at all of the beauty that surrounds you.* Look at the beauty of the sky and nature. There is nothing in nature, nothing in the natural order of creative process that is not beautiful. Isn't fire beautiful, even as it consumes? Isn't the wind, as it blows, a beautiful force even though it might feel destructive? Everything has its own beauty when you know how to see the beauty.

When you say the words of pain and fear to me, I say to you, *if you can look beyond all of your reactionary fears to an experience, there is always a beauty in the experience. If you can find the beauty in all experiences, you are then no longer subject to the illusion of pain and fear.*

You ask, "Is there anything to be gained from my perception of fear and pain on this planet?" Yes, all creative processes, expressions and experiences add to God. Everything is God. It is the judgments, perceptions and your fears that you transform. Transformation adds to God. It is not the experience nor the expression you transform; it is your perception of the experience that is transformed. As you heal your fear, you are transforming your perception of fear. You are now free to see the beauty of the experience.

What is there to be gained? You must accept that existence is a creative process forever creating. Pain and fear have become the creations you feel are threatening to you and your survival. When you no longer feel threatened by your perceptions of the experiences, you are no longer limited by them. When you are no longer limited, you are able to see their beauty.

Let us look at the disease of cancer you believe threatens your physical existence on the planet. The creation of cancer cells is such a powerful creative process that it overshadows other creations, e.g. what you believe to be healthy cells. What you believe to be a healthy cell is not truly healthy; it is filled with fear and has no power. If you were living from the power of your love, you would not experience the fear. Instead you would look for the beauty of the power of the creative process taking place. As you find the beauty in the creative process of a cancer cell, the beauty would enrich rather than destroy you.

The disease of cancer devours and destroys because the fear within you creates the destruction. The cancer will no longer devour and destroy when you see its beauty. The true power of love enriches the healthy cells and enhances your immune system. This is the best way in which I can explain transformation.

Because of your belief system of separation, your entire physical body is filled with fear. That is what you express.

Fear can be attacked very easily by anything that is more powerful. Love cannot be attacked, for love will embrace its attacker and bring out the beauty in the attacker. Instead of being attacked, suddenly the expansiveness of the union brings about a greater benefit for both.

The only purpose for fear and pain is expansive creation. Fear and pain are not allowing you to enjoy who you are and to continue your creative process to the fullest extent because they have limited you. You are afraid of your own self. When you can see all your creations in a different light, embrace them and love them, you live life from a different level. You prosper in all areas. Those around you begin to prosper and may never know why. Life is a beautiful expression of existence rather than a limiting experience.

- Suggested Meditation -
Creating With Love
Page 145

CHAPTER 8

The Message Is Simple—The Key To Expanding Is Unconditional Love

Simply open the door to all that you are by embracing All That Is as yourself with unconditional love. This is how you live in the oneness of life.

This is Jesus, and I come to you from the Love of the Father. It is not the physical incarnation as the man Jesus I would desire you to focus upon. Rather focus upon what I represent. I represent to you the consciousness of spirituality and the reality of Love that you are. When you become focused upon the persona of a person, you lose the true inner essence of the divinity living within the person. I say to you, *my message to the world is no different than the message within yourself. All are the expression of the Creator.*

I came to show you the way to find the divinity, the God-essence, the truth that lies within your own soul and Spirit. Look within yourself to find what is the truth.

See what lies within the inner realms of your Spirit. It seems so very difficult for humanity to know who they are, to remember the divinity that lies within them. You have forgotten how to live in the greatness, the richness and the fullness of your Spirit. The Creator created you in the fullness and totality of All That Is. Yet, my message to you is very simple.

The message simply is to lay aside all of the differences, release the pain, know your fears are not real and begin to look instead into the oneness of all life.

What does the oneness of all life mean to you? You judge all things by your perception of past experiences. If you stop and ask yourself the question, "What is the oneness of all life?", you would know it is God existing in all things.

God is life, and nothing exists outside the presence of this life force. In truth all is God and all is Love. The oneness of life is expanding your consciousness and entering without judgment into the consciousness of all existence.

If you feel the need to judge, then you are not entering into the Spirit that allows you to experience the oneness of life, for there is no judgment in the oneness. Judgment lies only in your individual perception of experiences. For if you did not have a perception of your experiences, you would have no need for judgment. Because of your judgments and fearful anticipation of future events, you do not allow yourself to expand in your consciousness. You are too restricted by your perception of past experiences and your judgments of those experiences.

How do you move beyond limitation into expansion? I would say to you, *find the place of Love within yourself that contains all possibilities.*

When I speak of Love, it seems as though the message is either received as too simple or too complex. Maybe you are afraid to love without judgments and reservations. Maybe it feels too simplistic to only love unconditionally. Yet, that is the beginning. That is your key to expansion. Love opens the door to truly recognizing you are All That Is. All That Is, is you. Until you choose to allow yourself to feel safe enough to expand your consciousness into All That Is, you will have no understanding of who you truly are. Since you have no concept of who you are, you feel threatened by what you do not know.

In order to be able to move into the consciousness of All That Is, you must let go of your judgments. This is the only way to open the door of Love and truth.

You must accept All That Is without judgment, being able to embrace All That Is as yourself with unconditional love. You believe you cannot be safe in your world if you embrace that which creates pain. Yet, by embracing your perception of pain with unconditional love, you heal the perceptions creating the pain.

You heal the illusion, for in reality pain does not exist. Until you allow yourself to move into the expanded consciousness of the oneness of life and recognize it is you, you will neither see nor experience reality.

See yourself as the center of your universe. It is your energy sustaining All That Is. Anytime you feel isolated from love you become rebellious and frightened. Attempting to inflict an energy of pain and fear onto others allows you to be noticed only for the sake of being loved.

You are afraid to allow your consciousness to expand because you fear your own rebellion to the pain. This is the illusion. It is your belief in the pain and your fear of the power of true reality. Yet, the isolation of your consciousness is what allows the pain to continue. If you were to expand into your reality of Love, the pain and the rebellion would cease. Until you accept you are an immortal being expressing All That Is, it will be difficult for you to expand your consciousness into that awareness.

You have entered into an accelerated evolutionary stage. Therefore, the information given to you now is of a different nature from what you may have received in the past. Remember when you were in the first grade. You began by learning your ABCs, but by the time you reached college, you were far beyond where you were in the first grade. At this level of understanding you not only put sentence structure and paragraphs together, but you were telling stories.

At this time, it is of little benefit to teach you the ABCs. Humanity knows the ABCs, but they do not know how to put the sentence structure together. You know how to form the words, but you do not know how to make the words into a workable structure. Humanity does not yet know how to structure this new awareness into a format that gives them needed instruction for life. It is often difficult for this new format to take place because the awareness must be directed to a higher part of your consciousness, and you are not always in touch with this higher part of you.

It becomes a challenge to give you the concepts or sentence structure that you need and desire at this time when you only know words. The words do not form anything that becomes comprehensive to you. They are separated and isolated. You know what the words mean, but how do you join them together? How do you form a comprehensive sentence that will give life and reality to the words? Allow your consciousness to expand. You already know; you need only to remember.

Are there questions?

Q: We are in our incarnations, I am assuming, trying to evolve to become an ascended master. I would like to know how many ascended masters there are and are there levels to ascend to after the accomplishment of becoming an ascended master?

I would have to begin with your definition of ascended master because humanity assigns titles to an energy form in order to relate to the form. I am going to assume what is meant by ascended masters are primarily those souls for whom you have given titles.

At this time there are thirty-three ascended masters who work with humanity at various times. All of them are not on the same mission nor the same interaction with humanity. Many times you identify a form of energy in a way that your mind might understand and relate to the energy. Some of the forms are called angels or ascended master or extra terrestrials. There are other energies in the universe that perhaps you haven't named but identify them by their interaction with the planet.

There are many levels of existence and understanding

in all dimensions in the same manner as there are many levels of existence and understanding in your world. The very high masters have no way of entering the vibration that would interact with you but there are intermediaries.

I, Jesus, interact with you through a step down of vibrational rate. I interact through the humanity part of my consciousness, not through the part of my consciousness that is far beyond your understanding or your vibrational rate. So it is with many of those you think of as masters or higher beings.

Masters have all experienced physical existence. It is their human experience that interacts with humanity. The masters also possess a very high, expanded conscious level of existence far beyond the present level of human understanding. As you expand your consciousness, you begin to relate to the higher energy vibration of that same ascended master or energy form who is beyond its human experience. You then begin to experience your own higher consciousness, for, you see, there is nothing in the ascended masters' consciousness nor within their existence nor their energies that is not within you. They simply are more aware. They have opened their consciousness to a higher level of acceptance of reality.

This is what I help you to do. I take the part of consciousness that has experienced humanity and interact with you in a way that helps you open to higher levels of reality. I am no more than you. I simply am more aware of the totality of our existences, both yours and ours. Life is existence—existence that is forming, creating life continually. It is difficult to help you to understand using only your vocabulary and your thought patterns. You, yourself, must have that experience of consciousness.

When there are near-death experiences, you experience a higher consciousness of yourself. You interact with others at a higher conscious level. You touch into your own inner beauty and the beauty of all life. You return desiring to share your experience with others, but you only have your vocabulary. Vocabulary cannot begin to relate the beauty, greatness and awe of expanded consciousness. One must have the experience for one's self.

It is important for you to know you need not die. All you need to do is take some of the steps to remember your unlimited spiritual existence. Yet, those are large steps for you. It is a very large step for humanity to let go of judgments, to fully focus into this now moment, to embrace all of existence and to fully know it is them.

Pretend you are the creator of all you know, and it belongs to you. You are the creator of the planet and the stars, the angels and the murderer. Know you have created and expanded your universe with all these creations, and indeed, you are responsible for all you have created. Then what do you do to bring your universe into harmony? Do you inflict more pain upon your creations, do you isolate them, or maybe destroy them? You can't destroy them because once energy takes a creative form it cannot be destroyed. It will exist forever. It may change vibrational form, but it is impossible to no longer exist as a creation.

You are the creator. You are the one in charge. It is your

responsibility, and you want your world to be in harmony. How ever did you create this vast expanse? Indeed, if you are "the creator," then why are you so unaware of this truth? First, you must be willing to understand your creations because they are the reflection of you. Then, you must love them just because they exist. When you begin to accept and move into that awareness, your consciousness begins to expand. You see yourself for the master you truly are.

I wish to reach out to embrace you, to hold and love you trusting it is sufficient to stir an awakening in your soul. I desire to once again sit on a hillside and talk with you telling you stories to help you understand by using the vocabulary you know. Yet, all of your awakening still rests upon you. An ascended master can do nothing more than open the awareness that can then help you make the decision to choose to know who you are.

To thine own self be true and to your creations take responsibility and offer your love to all.

Q: In a previous statement you said, "I could not effect the mass consciousness." I don't understand how you could make this statement when I cannot imagine any other individual's life on this planet that has effected the masses in such a positive way as your life as Jesus. Can you please explain?

Let me start by explaining the mass consciousness. Mass consciousness is the collective thoughts, actions and words created while in physical incarnations on this planet. As your soul has returned time and time again, you have taken a part in creating mass consciousness. Humanity is a collective consciousness; all humanity is one.

You may not incarnate on this planet for a thousand years, but your creations have continued to create although you are not in a physical incarnation. They have continued to influence and be influenced by the mass consciousness. Therefore, when you return, your creations are not exactly as they were when you left. Rather they have become interwoven with like-kind creations, all collecting into a form called collective, mass consciousness. You are subject to the collective consciousness.

I was not a part of mass consciousness, I did not have previous creations of illusion left behind on this planet that became a part of the mass consciousness.

Let me speak to you of one of the times I was on the planet. It was a time written in your history. Yet, it was a time that seems to be shrouded in somewhat of a mystery. Using the name of Melchizedek, I entered into your world as a ruler. I came from a time and space outside of your known universe. I was not born by a natural birth process upon this planet. While I would be affected by the planet, I did not have previous creations that were a part of mass consciousness that would be with me if I had come by way of birth onto this planet. When I left, I very carefully insured that all creations created by my existence were transformed by the power of Love into reality. All of my creations were left in a divine providence to grow and expand only in the spiritual enlightenment of reality. Reality is never affected by illusion.

When I returned to your planet as Jesus, the energy surrounding my incarnation was only enlightenment. Enlightenment is far superior to ego creations, as the spiritual nature is always superior. I was not a part of the illusion of mass consciousness because I had left no previous creations of illusion on the planet.

You can always rise above the illusion of mass consciousness because the illusion is always subject to spiritual enlightenment. Think of the mass consciousness as layers of energy. Think of spiritual enlightenment as having the ability to move through the layers of mass consciousness to a higher plane of awareness. As spiritual enlightenment penetrates the mass consciousness, it will have a powerful effect just by the energy of reality passing through the layers of illusion of mass consciousness energy. I was not a part of the mass consciousness because I did not envelop myself in the mass consciousness. Because I was not subject to the mass consciousness, I could not change the mass consciousness

I could not and cannot heal your world. When I came as the man Jesus, I was not subject to human limitations. Because I was never subject to the limitations of the ego, I did not need to overcome them. I could not effect mass consciousness because I did not need to overcome the limitations of fear and illusion. Because of my physical presence 2,000 years ago, humanity began to awaken to a higher awareness of spirituality. The enlightenment of spiritual awareness will always provide a light to the soul. Your higher awareness effected mass consciousness.

My teaching, healing and the reality of Love detonated within the human Spirit, illuminating the heart and the soul, allowing your consciousness to explode into an expanded awareness even if only for a moment of time. The creation of expanded awareness became creator moving through mass consciousness. It began a spiritual awakening within humanity.

I had already established this layer of higher, spiritual awareness prior to the time I incarnated as Jesus. There was a collective body of energy established earlier known as Melchizedek. There was needed a collective body of energy to hold and to grasp the spiritual energy. If it were not there, the spiritual awareness would be dissipated into higher elements and would not remain to have an effect upon your planet. Without a creative source, energy does not take form but continually evolves to a higher dimension. Then there truly would be no effect upon your world.

When you ask me, "How was it I had not an effect upon the mass consciousness, yet, so many changes came about?" It was humanity who brought about the changes. It was the teachings, the demonstrations, the love sparking within the human soul once again and the ability among the masses to reach deep within and move into their own spirituality that effected mass consciousness.

There were twelve ascended masters (nonphysical, spiritual beings) who walked with the twelve disciples continuously empowering their efforts. It was the masters' assigned tasks to be with the disciples, to empower them and to keep within the disciples' consciousness the ability to remember transformation and ascension for as long as the disciples remained on the planet.

The human experience through the illusion of your frightened ego is so powerful the disciples faltered often. Even with my teaching, my presence on the planet, the demonstrations of miracles, and with the ascended masters working with them, the disciples did not always recognize the illusion to be illusion. Often times the message was not given correctly nor received correctly by the listener. However, if there is something in a spoken word or deed that sparks spiritual awareness, this becomes the beginning of transformation and ascension.

Q: Did you incarnate physically in any other lifetimes before or after your life as Jesus?

First of all let us speak about incarnations. When you speak of incarnations and your past lives, you again are touching into a small portion of your total experience in this universe. You are touching into the streams of energy of past lives most connected to your present life. In all reality, from your particular energy stream there are many different souls and those souls incarnate in different physical bodies, and yet, they all come from an individualized stream of energy. Think of your soul as one large circle and each incarnation as a small dot connected to other small dots, all making up the complexity known as soul, or individualized expression of God. Think of your soul beginning as a stream of energy pouring forth from a universal intelligent consciousness known as God. Know your soul is free to continue to create and expand.

When you ask me the question, did I incarnate on this planet before, the answer is yes. But never in a continuum that reproduced bringing cellular, emotional and mental vibrational energies into a subsequent incarnation.

I was at the beginning of your world and universe. I led a band of souls who created this particular universe, but I was not known as Jesus. I simply was consciousness. From our consciousness, we simply thought and thought set energy into motion forming vibrational patterns. These vibrational patterns became self-aware existences on your planet. As creators, those existences we had spawned by our thought became a part of our consciousness. This self-aware existence contained all the creative ability and freewill of the Creator. Each self-aware existence was free to grow and create with total freewill choices. This gave the uniqueness of individuality to your universe.

I first incarnated very early in the first stages of humanity. Others and myself have incarnated from time to time when humanity needed guidance. Many attempted to infuse guidance by intermingling and intermarrying. I returned again in the earliest time of recorded history. I came in positions of authority, bringing an order to the world on your planet. I, then, returned again as a prophet. Finally, I returned as Jesus. My incarnation was not from a genetic pool or cellular code but from a different stream of consciousness. The man Jesus was very unique. So when you ask if I have incarnated, the consciousness has been here in many forms and in other lifetimes, but the man Jesus was a pure conscious stream that was not limited by the experiences of those previous lifetimes.

Have I returned again? No. Humanity has been given much information and the information has been disseminated. Other masters have come and given information and that information, too, has been disseminated. What will you do with what you presently know?

The presence of one who you would seek to heal your world, a Savior, is very temporal. The healing process within yourself is eternal.

Q: You mentioned as Jesus you came in the purest energy stream of your true self. Are we allowed or capable of doing the same?

Yes, but your energy stream may be different from mine. Your origination, as you began to be creative process through the various modalities of creations, are different from mine. All that you have brought into the purity of your energy stream, being without fear and without limitation, is likely different from my energy stream. It does not mean one is greater than the other but different. The pure modality of who you are is so wrapped in your belief of illusion that you are unable to express it in the human body form at this time.

Can you express in the pure energy of your true self? Of course you can. Can your energy stream incarnate apart from your mass conscious creations and your past lives? No, it cannot. You have chosen those past lives to have those experiences and to create those creations. If, indeed, you were at this time to incarnate from the pure energy stream I speak of, you would still immediately be encompassed with all of your creations from previous incarnations on this planet.

You must realize the reality of the **NOW** moment, transforming your creations. This is what humanity is now doing. You are becoming aware of your spirituality, of this higher part of yourself, of your ability to transform your creations by beginning to realize that the key to transformation is love. As you take those steps, the beautiful, pure energy stream begins to express through you. That is God in totality, omnipotence expressing through your soul, omnipotent energy stream of all power, All That Is without fear or limitation.

God is Love giving of itself continually, creating beauty and light. Give of yourself always, continually emptying yourself that you might become more than you are presently.

The more you give of yourself unconditionally the more you pull in a beautiful stream of self-expression, of creative process that gives of itself. When you are afraid to give of yourself, when you lock yourself away, there is no opportunity for you to become aware of the greater, higher part of yourself. The higher part of yourself does not know how to isolate or encapsulate itself on the planet. It only knows how to continue to flow in a manner of self-giving and creative process.

If you wonder why you create amiss, if you say I would never create "that" in my life, then know you are creating from your limited awareness and previous creations that are also very limited and narrow.

You ask, "Can you come to the planet as I came to the planet?" In a simplified answer, I would say, *not at this time, but it does not mean you cannot be even greater than I.* It does not mean you have a lesser stream of energy. It very simply means, transform your creations by the power of Love. Live from your spiritual essence. Love unconditionally, and you will then create from the stream of pure creative energy. You shall do great things for yourself and for others.

Q: You mentioned that our incarnations in this world are but a small portion of our total experience in this universe. Could you describe what our other experiences would be?

When I speak of incarnation, I am speaking only of your human form as your conscious mind knows it to be. That form is a small part of you because you are in all things.

The universe supports an expansive, creative process. You are a participant in the continuous creation of new worlds and planets. You are also a participant in experiencing those new worlds and planets that are experiencing the birth of new life and in exploring what is unknown to you in your conscious mind on this planet.

You are All That Is, and All That Is, is you. The universe abides within you, and you abide within the universe. There is no separation between you and All That Is.

You may ask, "Why am I not consciously aware of my total existence?" At this time the division stands for several reasons. First, you do not wish to transport your present, self-imposed limitation to the creative process beyond your galaxy because the entire universe would become a limited experience of fear, limitation and imprisonment. Second, you have erected your own barrier, division or line of awareness you do not choose to cross. Third, there is a part of you who knows you are unlimited, knows you are God and that you are perfect in every way. That higher awareness is part of you and is always with you residing as a human being on your planet. It is the same part of your soul that explores the beyond. Your higher self is connected to this inner consciousness and flows back and forth on waves of energy. It is God awareness. Your consciousness, as you understand and know your consciousness to be, has no understanding of such a connection. When I say to you, *you are more than you know, you are more than your incarnations, I am merely saying to you, you are All That Is within this universe, and this universe is totally within you.*
All possibilities exist within as they are expressed

without. A possibility may simply be a new color. It may be expressed as a beautiful new sound. Perhaps a new physical form begins to take shape. The possibility may be the wonder of creating a new world.

You are the supreme creation and the embodiment of all possibilities. There is nothing you are not aware of that is any greater than you. It is your self-imposed limitation that does not allow you to realize this truth.

Q: If anger is an expression or result of fear, please explain what happened in the temple when the money changers were given a reprimand. The Bible tells us you expressed anger. Is that a misinterpretation?

As events are retold, they carry with them the perception of the person as the person recalls what took place.

I can never be angry with my brothers and sisters who are in such pain. Why would I be angry with any of you? What is there for me to be angry about? A temple worship? How important is a temple worship or any form of ritual? I feel great compassion and love. My heart felt the pain of humanity while I was on the planet, for I could feel your pain. The pain was so heavy. Why would I be angry? Your souls feel frightened and small. You believed you could do so little to rescue yourself from the sea of mass consciousness that had created and sustained such pain.

*I would never be angry with my brothers
and sisters. For when you have
understanding of their pain, there is no need
for anger. You have nothing to be angry
about. It is as though the person you love
the very most is in the deepest pain you
could imagine, and you are angry at that
individual for expressing his or her pain.
Think of that for a moment.*

Think of the person you love the most and think of them
in the deepest pain you could imagine. Would you be angry at them? No, you love them. You desire to free your
loved one from the pain. You feel compassion; therefore,
you are not angry. If you in your limitation of pain can feel
such a desire, do you not know I, too, would feel compassion and love?

*There isn't a soul on this planet my love
does not reach. I love in a way you cannot
know for I do not judge you. As long as you
have judgments, your judgments will
restrict your love. Judgment limits love and
diminishes it for all.*

If you were God, what would you do? Would you destroy your planet? Would you sit idly by and see a beautiful

creation in such pain? Would you try to find ways to help? Are you a parent? If you are a parent and your children are in pain, what would you do? Would you destroy them because they are in pain? Would you find a place of torment in which to place these beautiful children who are in such pain so you could torment them for their pain? Is that logical even to your limited thinking?

Think of the omnipotent God, Creator of all. As God, you empowered your creations with your power, but the creations have forgotten. You cannot take this power from your creations because it is who they are. They must become aware of this power for themselves. That is the way it is. What would you do? Would a part of yourself enter into your children's world and show them Love? Would you teach them about beauty, harmony, joy, peace and the reality of Love? Would you show them how to enjoy their lives and heal their pain? Yes, you would do this. You are God, and you are the child.

You were created from the same God consciousness as I. We are no different. You have become almost totally blinded by your belief in your separateness. Until you remove the wrapping of this belief and know All That Is—is you, you will not heal. You will never know the beauty of expanded consciousness. Yet, it is who you are; you have only forgotten. Do not look to me as greater than you; I am you. We are not different. All life is one.

Q: Many people on our planet see things as good and evil, while others see all things in life as an expression of divinity. The latter see evil as an expression of divinity that has just forgotten it is an expression of divinity. If you could give some spiritual insight, what would you say about evil?

Evil is your interpretation of your fears. Since you feel out of control, there must be a power beyond your control that has created these fears—the evil power. By the thoughts of many, such an energy is created and then those souls give a name to the creation, but it is their creation. The power of this creation is sustained only as long as it is fed by the belief. You need not be a part of that creation nor a part of the energy sustaining the creation. It is only if you have the need to interpret your fears as an evil, outside energy, do you sustain the mass conscious interpretation of that energy to be Satan or demons.

All acts of disharmony are acts of fear. Therefore, if you believe in evil, all fear is evil to you. You have degrees of evil. When you think something is not really evil, you may only call it bad. When it is a great fear, then it is evil. Yet, it is all in the family of fear. You perceive evil to be anything that is a threat to your perception of your safety. As long as you choose to sustain such a belief, the energy will affect you.

When you understand evil is only your own fears, when you do not sustain the energy, when you no longer believe in the energy, when you no longer give power to the energy, it has no affect upon you because it no longer is a part of your existence. It may still be an active part of mass consciousness but without any affect upon you. Individualized consciousness of the reality of Love is always greater than the mass consciousness belief in fear and illusion; remember that.

You must remove your thoughts, your energy and your belief totally from a creation of illusion, and then you are no longer subject to the belief or the power of that belief.

This is possible, but it isn't just by making the statement, "Well, then I don't believe in _____." It is the healing process that removes the belief. The detachment from mass consciousness does not occur by desire alone. You must actively choose to trust in your deep, inner, spiritual awareness and the divinity in all life; honor the divinity without judgments, and allow God to express through you with Love. It is only as you heal, as you move into the reality of Love, as you judge not, and as you let go of the power of perception of your experiences, as you begin to know you are safe that you withdraw your energy from the belief of evil. It is not just saying, "I do not believe in evil." It is by healing your fears that the energy streams feeding the belief in evil dissolve or are transformed. This allows freedom from the belief.

You are free; you need not be subject to any belief system except your own.

Q: Is the Bible absolute or infallible to error since humans wrote it and have since translated it into many languages?

There is an essence of truth in all your holy books. This essence of truth is contained not only in the Bible but in all of the holy books written with the intent to help you remember and grow spiritually.

Read the Bible or any other holy book from your Spirit, not your mind, asking your own internal guidance to give to you the essence of the spiritual truth contained therein.

There is then much to be profited by these beautiful, spiritual writings. However, if you are going to read the writings to take a complete and literal understanding of every word and story, then you must know these writings are not absolute.

Many of your current holy works were written with good intentions, but many of the ancient manuscripts were lost and/or forgotten. Many were handed down from the stories that were told and retold. The stories were written as they were remembered, or they were written from the perspective and viewpoint of the writer. However, there is an essence of truth that lies within the writings. Read from your Spirit. Find **YOUR** truth in these holy books. The same is true when reading any of the beautiful teachings of many wise souls.

When you take the essence of the truth within your soul and Spirit, the truth shall set you free.

If any writing or source of information brings a bondage to you, it is not truth. Truth will always set you free. Truth will always uplift.

Remember there is never a bondage or fear in truth. There will never be a doubt or a question where truth lies when it resonates within your soul. If the writing or information contain many rules, rituals and regulations, it has little to do with truth; it is bondage. There are no rituals needed. Rituals further bind you into a restrained understanding of your consciousness.

- *Suggested Meditation* -
Golden Light of Transformation
Page 141

CHAPTER 9

A Bright Tomorrow

Within your soul there is hope for your world.
As you share your love, blessings and peace with all
of humanity, so it is that you bring the light, wisdom
and the divinity of the Creator into everyday life.

This is Jesus. I enter your presence in Love, for the reality of Love is the only power that resides within my Spirit the same as within your Spirit. Think of yourself as having been born in a sea of water. Perhaps you are one of several hundred new life forms having come forth from an existing life form. You are small, helpless and subject to so many dangers. If you survive at all, it is a miracle but you do. Slowly you grow and develop. You begin to take a larger shape and form. Your form has discovered more distinguishing powers within itself, and you now better understand your environment. You understand that sometimes you become the predator, sometimes you are the protector, and sometimes you simply reflect the awesome beauty of life. Reflecting beauty is really what your existence is intended to be.

You were spawned from an energy stream that sent out billions of energy streams. You took all types of shapes and forms, understandings and knowings. Every tiny cell went forth complete and total within itself. You can be the beauty of life, the predator or the protector of life. You have survived in your world.

You are now grown up. You understand life. You may at times be confused by your world and your known forms of life, but basically you understand it. Somewhere deep inside you know you are the life force that sustains your existence, and you know you can be any expression you choose to be. You know this. However, you allow your thoughts and reflections of your outer world to be your truth. Forgotten is your ability to allow the unlimited you to come forth, express and play.

You are the light ray that goes forth and dances with life in your world. As the ray dances, it embraces various partners here and there and takes them into that beautiful light which then allows the partners to go on their various journeys. That is what I would like to challenge you to do. Let the light be your guide and let it dance through life.

Don't go through life with a shovel digging a ditch and working so hard at trying to explore how deep you can go. You can never go deep enough because what you seek is not in the depths. You will find your delight in dancing on the rays of light. It is allowing your Spirit to express. It is trusting your immortality. It is trusting that the real you exists outside of time and space and that you are not limited by either. It is trusting in the totality of who you are.

That is all I did and that is all you can do. Be the light that you are.

The New Resurrection

Within your soul there is hope for your world. As you share your love, blessings and peace with all of humanity, so it is that you bring the light, wisdom and the divinity of the Creator into everyday life. The lofty ideas of intellectual humanity are not the gateway to heaven, for the intellectuals will seek many avenues within their reasoning powers attempting to bring to their domains the peace and joy they seek. Peace and joy are not to be found in your halls of reason. They are to be found in the light and beauty of your soul, your Spirit and your heart.

Peace and joy are not to be discovered for you alone. You must share your truth and your love with your brothers, sisters and every life form.

There is a light radiating in every living thing. When you, my brothers and sisters, can see the radiating light within all others, you know you are upon your path to enlightenment.

Turn your faces upward into the Love of the Father even as the flowers reach to the sun. Feel yourself being nurtured and know it is truly happening. As you lie in a very quiet, undemanding and yet expecting bed of hope, know you are safe. Life without hope can become very destructive.

Life without joy is like going into a dark cave feeling your way around the parameters.

You search for something to show you the way into the light, and the way into the light is to be the light.

To be the light is not to be a passive being on your planet. To be the light is to activate your inner truth.

You then awaken the reality of Love and joy that resides within each soul. To be the light is to connect with the higher divine power that radiates throughout every existence. It is a time in your world to resurrect the truth, love, light, joy, harmony and peace. It is a time to be your brother's keeper. It is a time to extend your hand to the one you would normally walk by without noticing. It is a time to be the light and to see the light in all others.

The light is shining upon your planet and your world. It is a mobile light; it is not fixed. If it passes by your way, will you recognize the light when you see it? You say I want to expand, and I say to you, *will you recognize it when it comes? Will you recognize the light as it comes into your presence?* The light will not be announced by a great proclamation; it shall come in the gentleness of the rain, in the warmth of the sun and the beauty of your heart. All of this is the resurrection, the light, the truth and the way.

Be the light, and you shall recognize the light. Recognize the light in all others, and together you shall light your world. As the light begins to multiply and radiate, it dispels the fear of darkness. For just a moment allow me to radiate to you the love that I feel so compassionately for you my brothers and sisters. Open your hearts and share with me the beauty of who you are.

I am always with you. I shall always be with you. My love shall always encompass you. It is not by your good deeds that I love you. It is as you open and allow yourself to receive the love we become one. I strengthen your faith. I walk by your side. I am no different from or greater than you. Journey with me down your path of light, and I will be faithful in staying with you. Walk with me down the dusty roads and into the corners of those who are experiencing suffering and pain, and we will bring light to heal the pain. We will do it together. I give to you my blessing, peace, joy, and love.

Q: How much longer before humanity will awaken?

You are truly about to enter a new age. You are already in the evolutionary processes of this age. In this age, you will escalate in your own understanding and expand faster than you have for perhaps tens of thousands of years. It will depend upon whether your spiritual nature becomes your guide or your technological age becomes your guide.

The technology you have developed is a great satisfier to your analytical mind. There is nothing wrong with technology if it is not your God. You are becoming more and more a slave to your technologies. Whether it is in your toys, work or what you perceive to be the needs of life. You are becoming consumed by the fascination of your technologies. As time continues to contract, you will find you must make choices as to how to use your time. Technology should never consume more energy than spirituality in a society.

When I speak of spirituality, I am saying, *always honor the Spirit of all life, be it humanity, an animal, a plant or an idea or thought. See the divinity in all existence. Do not allow technology to dehumanize your soul.*

I think perhaps one of your greatest challenges in this age of information is how easily information can be accessed. Because there is so much information available to you now, and it is so accessible to you, your focus is on the consumption of information. I am not saying to you to abandon your technology and go back to the middle ages; I am just asking, *will your technology, spirituality, or age of information be your God?*

Now, for those who will make technology their God, they are going to be trapped in their world of technology, and they won't have any idea of the possibilities of where the entrapment will take them. Such a journey will fascinate the mind even more. For now technology has acquired an energy and life form of its own, and it generates more technology at lightning speed. The information then flows into your mind through the energy corridors, and you are fascinated more and more. New technology is a force of its own now and is entrenched, glorified and fascinated with its own energies. It is fed and sustained by the energy of your thoughts.

Those souls whose energy focus allows will become deeper and deeper entrapped in technology. Those who seek their own spiritual nature can still use and enjoy all the wonders of the technology recognizing it only as a benefit to life but not becoming entrapped by a need or dependency upon the same. I do not say abandon your technology; I do say don't let it become your God.

As your consciousness expands, you will begin to recognize how to go beyond technology. You will recognize it to be the primitive tool it truly is. You will learn how to access the information simply by thought processes versus using technology, and you'll not be bound by the information nor the technology.

So when you ask what is humanities' evolutionary path, I see two paths. The choice is one for each individual soul. I can tell you both paths will accelerate extremely fast. They have already begun to do so. Do you not already feel the time crunch and feel something is happening?

You will see the masters and feel the wisdom of the wise souls. People will stand before you and disappear. Miracles as you perceive miracles to be, will be performed. You will see spiritually-aware people manifest objects from pure energy.

Those souls will likely be perceived as a very large threat to people who are involved with technology because the technologists cannot control the spiritually-minded souls but neither can the technologists destroy them. The vibrations of the truly spiritually-minded individuals will be such that they will walk through a crowd and never be touched. Those who depend upon their technology will not be able to destroy the spiritually-awakened souls. The technologists' fear will create the perceived need for more technology and deeper fear. Eventually, you will have two separate worlds; one world will be controlled by fear and the other world will radiate with love, joy, harmony and peace. This may be your concept of heaven and hell as your prophets saw and taught the masses.

No matter which path you take eventually there will come a time when you will once again return to the full consciousness from which you came or reawaken to your full, spiritual awareness. The more souls who expand their awareness, the faster you will evolve. The two worlds will one day become unified once again as all souls awaken to the truth of their reality.

Q: Jesus, you tell us to be the light that we are and to trust that we are the light, this seems overwhelming at times. We seem to struggle to be the light and being the light should not be a struggle. How can we lessen the struggle?

How does the human soul allow itself to move from its fear, for that is, indeed, your question? When there is struggle, there is fear, which is your belief in the illusion of your separation from your Creator. Light is the first creation from the sound vibration placed upon energy that brings about form. You are light; you can be no other. And when I say be the light, this means to allow yourself to Be that which you are. Be that, allow that.

The only reason you would struggle is because your fear and limitation deny what you are. They deny you are light, and, therefore, you feel you must search for the light and in searching for the light, you feel you cannot find it.

Light is not to be found in struggle; struggle is of illusion and fear. It is not to be found in some deep-rooted search. It must just Be.

Light must just shine.

You do not struggle and search and work at allowing the light of your beautiful sun to shine; it just shines upon your Earth and so it is with your own being. It is the result of what it is. Your light shines because it is the result of who you are. You need only to allow it to shine. How do you do that?

Well, you do it by accepting and becoming aware you

are All That Is, and when you accept this and embrace all things, then, the light begins to shine forth—it is in the quietness of the Spirit, it is not in the struggle of life. The struggles of life will never bring forth light, but the quietness of the Spirit will.

When you allow yourself to come to a place of calm, peace and trust, you begin to feel the power of all that you are.

And as you feel that power, you begin to let it radiate. You don't question it. You don't begin to try to deny it; it just radiates through. And the power it radiates through is the light and then you are the light. It doesn't matter what you are doing. You may simply be sitting, you may be having a conversation, you may be in nature, you might be doing a menial task, you may be very deep in concentration, you may be at your job or career, you may be caring for another, it matters not what you are doing. It is in allowing the quietness of the Spirit that the light shines forth.

When you feel fear, when you feel struggle, when you feel weary, realize those are all signs that you are living your life from illusion, living your life by denying the power that you are, denying the light that you are. Stop for a moment and allow the Spirit to begin to flow—just allow the peace of who you are, allow the beauty. You can do nothing to make those things happen. You must step aside and allow, for it is a power that is far greater than the consciousness of your mind could ever produce.

Q: How can an organization that is dedicated to spiritual evolution continue to grow and expand?

Organization is not what I would attempt to direct on your path. Those are choices you make upon your path and own destination of life. I connect with your love to empower you. It is the love that I wish to convey to humanity.

When you ask, I will certainly empower all you do that conveys the message of love to others. It is important that the message of truth, love, harmony, joy and peace be heard and lived. But you see the words are very shallow if the energies and vibrations of your beings do not match your words.

There is no power that is separate from the divinity within you whereby changes or healings are effected. It must be totally all things coming together in harmony and unity. It is the harmony and the unity that I would embrace within you, my friends and within all others. Such, I find, to be the importance of life. Go forth and embrace all that will bring to you the remembrance of who you are.

Q: Jesus, you said I am with you, and I shall always be with you, and I walk with you upon your path. When people ask for your help, how can you be with so many people all over the world at the same time?

You try to restrict the consciousness of creativity to your physical environment. Even in your physical environment can you not think of a friend while, perhaps, repairing an automobile. Your mind is thinking of your friend while repairing the automobile simultaneously. Can you not look into the sky and think of something else as well, even though it seems these are separate activities, it is a simultaneous action that is taking place. If you wish to remove the equation of the illusion of time from the situation, you can also recognize that without time you are all things in all places, doing all things, experiencing all things, being all things.

I do not live in the construct of your time and space. I do not exist within that dimension by that limitation, and therefore, as I think, so it is. As your thought comes to my state of consciousness, so a thought goes forth. It is not difficult for me to have millions of conscious interactions because it is a state of consciousness. An example would be just as you can be a male, a friend, a farmer, a father, a brother, so I can be a vast state of consciousness. When you call, I hear.

You think of me as the limited being in physical form who walked the planet. The limited physical form is not the consciousness of my soul. I interact with you from the humanity part of my consciousness but that part of me is not limited as you are limited by your physical existence.

You must I suppose, by faith, accept that as I say to you, *I am with you always, so it is.* Because my consciousness has so interacted with your universe and particularly your world, it is within me; it is a part of me. Each soul is a part of me as you are a part of all others. Therefore, I do not have to reach far to interact with any part of your world.

I hear the cry of a bird. I hear the screams that are silent to you in the forest. They are within me as I am within them. Because your consciousness is not as expanded as mine at this time, you do not know these things. They take place, they are within you, but you do not know. You are unaware.

I am aware and in that awareness it is the love that goes forth. Love serves to sustain the life force of existence in your world, and it is the love that is always sent forth to heal the pain. But when you are consciously connecting with my consciousness, then you become very clearly aware of the love I give to you, and when you ask for my help, then I am free to empower you in ways you have not, yet, understood.

- Suggested Meditation -
High Pastures
Page 133

PART II

Meditations

Meditation is an active form of calming and quieting the mind. Because our logical minds are continuously analyzing, conceptualizing, categorizing and judging what they perceive, this constant activity blocks or hinders our efforts to contact the deep, inner knowing that each of us possess.

By quieting the mind, a doorway to our inner knowing begins to open. In the quiet moments, we can literally hear, sense, feel or intuitively know the answers to the most perplexing questions.

Because of the important role meditation plays in assisting us to journey inward, thereby discovering our own inner truth, the following meditations were given by Jesus.

CHAPTER 10

High Pastures Meditation

I invite you to come with me up to the "high pastures" where the air is pure, and the grass is green and sweet. Sit with me in the silence of the wind. Refresh in the meadow dotted throughout with beautiful, healing flowers of every color and hue. Feel the warmth of the sun as it rises in the sky or join me in the moonlight of the night sky sprinkled with twinkling stars. Here I will share with you the richness of the love of the universe.

You may stay with me for moments, hours, days or in a timeless eternity. The choice is yours alone. In the "high pasture" the illusion of fear and worry disappear. You know the truth of the unlimited, abundant world in which you live. In the "high pasture" the snow falls pure and fresh, cleansing the soul and refreshing the Spirit. You remember the beauty and Love that you truly are. Often times this frightens you for you do not recognize this Love, beauty and power are truly the reality of your soul. Your ego desires to run back to the safety of the lower pasture.

I invite you to stay forever in the "high pasture" of life. Many, however, are drawn back into the lower pastures of illusion. They experience the beauty of the "high pasture," but the lower pastures call them back. The ego understands how to survive in the lower pasture.

Sadly, I watch many return after only a brief moment of time in the presence of their Love, beauty and power. It would seem the remembrance of life in the lower pasture is so familiar the ego feels like a stranger in the presence of the awesome soul that, indeed, you are.

Although the grass is sparse and brown, although there are only a few healing flowers in the lower pasture, you have learned to survive there. The ego knows how to struggle through receiving the limited good the lower pasture can offer.

Rest assured that the "high pasture" is your home. The more you return to the abundance of the "high pasture", the more you shall remember it is your rightful birthright here on your beautiful planet Earth.

It was always meant for you to live in the "high pasture" of life. It shall always remain your home. Return as you choose. Bring with you the fellow travelers you meet along life's road. Let them know there is a "high pasture" always available for their return home.

I leave you in love. I am Jesus

CHAPTER 11

The Light Of Love Meditation

I join with you in the light of all that you are, and I speak to the light. I speak a command to the light that it come forth and envelop all your creations. As the light that is you shines brighter and brighter, it dissolves into nothingness all you have created that is less than your reality.

The light surrounds all creations of anger, frustration, sorrow, depression and fear. The illusion of all creations having not been created in love dissolve in the light of your reality. As of this moment, you are free of the illusion of those creations.

As the reality of your creations become more distinct, as you begin to see your beauty and Love, you recognize all that you are. You connect with all you have created. You may recognize color and shape. You may feel emotion; you may become aware of past lives or future lives. You are now totally aware of your creations.

As you view your creations, recognize this is your creative power but not your reality. Your creations are beautiful, and you did a good job. This gives you a feeling of worth, individuality, recognition and yes, a sense of power.

Therefore, you now recognize there is no need for control nor manipulation, for beauty is created from the power of love. Love does not control, love does not manipulate, and love leaves no room for fear. The light of who you are envelops all you have created. The light gives a clearer definition to your creations. The light gives you direction in your life.

At this very moment, you have an awareness of how to direct your life in the most positive, loving manner. You realize you have created many paths you no longer choose to follow. You now allow those paths to dissolve. They disappear, and as you look ahead, you see a brilliance of beauty beyond any brilliance you have ever known. You move down the path toward that brilliance.

The more you move into the brilliance, the more you realize the beautiful brilliance is you. The brilliance is who you truly are. All the creations of illusion dim by comparison to the reality of who you really are. You now have the awareness of your true creative power.

You did not remember who you were. You have been creating from the shadow of the brilliance but not from the brilliance itself. As you enter the brilliance and merge with the beauty and love of this beautiful light, you feel the love as it vibrates through every cell in your body. Your mind understands with a new awareness. You recognize the reality of who and what you are. You are Love and that is all there is.

With this awareness, all illusion melts around you. The reality of your creations emerge forming a beautiful pool of rainbow colors. You look at the rainbow colors and realize they would not exist had you not created them. Their beauty begins to expand; they unite in a harmony of color and melody. That is the beauty of creation.

In the midst of the beauty of color, music and harmony, you see other brilliant lights. You recognize the light is truth; the light is Love. Even the beauty created from the rainbow of colors dims by comparison to the brilliant lights that come forth. The light is the reality of All That Is.

Each light, including your own, begins to merge together into the most beautiful, sparkling, brilliant glow. As this beautiful, sparkling, brilliant glow of all the lights join together, it lights the universe, and it lights your world. It brings reality to your understanding. Reality is as the light is. Love is as you are. With that awareness, I leave you in a few moments of silence. Experience that awareness........

Take your mental consciousness deeper, deeper and deeper into the light until there is no mental awareness. Your consciousness is merged with the reality of All That Is.........

Return your consciousness to the present moment knowing you can return to your brilliant light at will, knowing it is only your awareness of all that you are, knowing that in the stillness you become one with the brilliance. Feel your soul express your totality of Love. Let your mind be the spectator, not the dictator.

As your conscious awareness returns, you now know the brilliance of your soul and Spirit. That is your reality. As your consciousness moves through the rainbow of colors, you recognize a part of you is trapped by the illusion and moves into illusion once again. You also realize you no longer need to be a part of the illusion entrapment. In the past it was your choice to be entrapped by the illusion, but now you realize the power of your reality of Love.

With that awareness you feel a freedom. You are now more aware of who you are. You are freer than you were a few moments ago. There is now a slight distance between you and the illusion you believed was the reality of your life. You now have the freedom of choice. Your soul is aware of its own brilliance, of its reality, of its power.

Each time you move into the reality of the brilliance

there is an awareness that grows. This awareness allows you to create from reality. You are no longer creating from the fear of illusion. Your creations of reality express in your life, your world, your universe giving forth perfect harmony, love, joy, and peace. Be all that you are. Be the Love that you are. I am Jesus.

CHAPTER 12

Expanding Your Consciousness Meditation

Can you for even one brief moment take your consciousness with me? Step out of time and space. Be all things, all possibilities. Step beyond your mind and move into a space of the eternal now moment with me. In this eternal now moment with me have one single thought—the one single thought of life. See only life, the expression of the eternal God. What is it? It is beyond all possible thoughts that you might have. Feel your own energy at this moment begin to expand. Feel yourself begin to expand and expand, moving into all possibilities. As you do this, there are no judgments, no limitations, no time, and no space—only the eternal moment. You are the eternal moment, my friend. This is your true existence. This is the expression of life, and you are that expression.

Bring your awareness back to the physical. Just by the act of your expansion, you have changed your entire molecular form. You are not the same as you were a moment ago. Your consciousness has expanded. I would invite you to forever see yourself as a beautiful expression of life and Love.

Love yourself as you are. Love, honor and respect your fellow, human traveler and all life. My friend, by this act of love, you are on the way to the most beautiful expression of existence ever known. Take your brother and sister by the hand and always uplift them, never pull them down. For in the act of pulling down those you interact with, you pull yourself down, but in the act of lifting up your fellow human beings, so you lift up yourself. You lift up God and you lift up your universe.

Understand the pain the ego has created. Understand the perceptions that keep your soul and others in bondage. Allow yourself to rise above those perceptions, and I will say to you, *you walk with the masters my friend, for that is where the masters walk.* I honor your love, your beauty and your existence. I leave you in the Love of the Creator, and I am Jesus.

CHAPTER 13

Golden Light Of
Transformation Mediation

As you quiet your mind, surround your heart with a brilliant, gold light. This beautiful, gold light is you. Set aside any thoughts of your body and your mind. Just for a moment be the gold light. You are pure. You are complete. You can feel your beauty and your Love. This is your God-energy; this is the spark of life that is the perfection in all the universe expressed in so many ways.

As you feel the beautiful, gold spark of awareness within you, the same awareness within me reaches out and unites in oneness with you. The spark becomes a little larger and a little brighter, but it has not changed; it is your divine essence. You are allowing the purity of the God-essence to flow within you.

Allow the light to expand until it completely surrounds you. Allow this beautiful divine essence to touch all you create and all souls who are in your life. All become one. In the purity of the Love of this golden light, without the clutter and clatter of life, I speak to you, my brothers and my sisters.

We journey back to a simpler time when you knew who you were. You knew the reality of your Love, and it was your guiding light. Feel it now. Feel the Love that you are. Feel the peace, the greatness, the joy, as you recognize the oneness of all life. You are part of every existence, of all creation on your planet and beyond. All creations are a part of you. All blend in harmony, in peace, with a song of joy in the perfect Love of the Creator.

As you move deeper and deeper into your center of Love and beauty, the love flows through every part of your being. You are purifying, cleansing, transforming and perfecting all you touch. My beloved, that is what I did when I was on Earth and it is no different from what you feel at this moment. Allow the perfect you that you are to permeate through everything it touches. You shall purify, transform and make perfect all your creations.

Those that come into your energy field feel what they do not understand, but they are drawn to it because it is the reality of who they also are. You are showing them the way home. You are sending them love. You are being Love.

I am walking among you even now. You can feel the hem of my garment as it passes you, but I am no different from you. Simply allow the perfection of your being to radiate as I did. That is the message to the people. When you walk in peace, and in love, life is a wonderful new window of beauty. People are drawn to you. You need not determine their needs. Your love will penetrate and heal their needs in that it helps them to recognize who they truly are.

Stay in this energy of love that you have created from the meditation. You are enveloped in the pure essence of Love. Feel the transforming power of this Love. How does it affect your life? You need not struggle with life. You sometimes think you have to struggle, you sometimes do. But I say to you, *life is who you are, and struggle is your imperfect perception of who you think you are.*

I ask you for a moment to bring one situation, one person or one circumstance to your mind that appears to be a problem for you. I ask you to think of every aspect of the problem that irritates you, angers you, inconveniences you and frustrates you. How bad is the problem? How bad is the person? How bad is the circumstance? Now, drop the problem at your feet and send the golden light of Love to transform it into the purest gold. The problem has the same quality, but it has become shiny and bright. Now, see the gold melting, and allow the problem to mingle with the gold, becoming purified. Out of that purity shines forth a brilliant, beautiful light of love. The light of love showers down upon you.

Allow the purification, for if you hold onto the problem as it first seemed to be, you will bring back the sludge and heaviness of the problem, and it remains a part of you. You can repeat these steps again and again until only the purest of Love remains. When it is pure, you will see the beauty of the creation. You will no longer see from your imperfect perception which is why at first it seemed a problem.

As I walked your planet, I saw the pains, sorrows and pleasures of the people. As I reached out and touched each one, I could feel the emotions of each person. I say to you, *at this very moment if you reach out, you can feel the emotions of the people in your life, for you are no different than me.* If an emotion is filled with pain, you have the ability to help transform the pain with your love. You are all here working together in a unit to find your way back to the purity of who you are, to remember and recognize the truth of who you are. The reality of your soul and Spirit are not lost. It is only that you do not remember. You are light and Love. I am Jesus.

CHAPTER 14

Creating With Love Meditation

For a moment relax and extend your palms upward. Allow the purest and highest spiritual energy of the universe to flow down through your spiritual, crown chakra located at the crown of your head. Allow the energy to flow through every cell of your body, pouring forth as an expression of light through both of your palms. Feel the energy as it flows through the palms of your hands and goes forth. See the energy as your creative power. As the energy of creation from your spiritual self flows from your palms, give it shape and form for the higher good of all.

Hold your world in light and love. Allow this love to flow over all your world, allow it to flow to every expression of creation. Allow the power of your love to enfold and envelop every experience that is taking place on your world at this time. See the beauty of life. See yourself as light. See yourself dancing on the rays of light. Be one with the light and the awareness of the glory and beauty you have created.

I leave you in the Love that you are, the light and the beauty. I leave you in the Love of the Father that abides eternally in you, and I am Jesus.

CHAPTER 15

The Healing Power Of A
Rose Petal Meditation

For a moment relax and extend your palms upward. I am placing in the palm of your right hand the energy essence of one rose petal. BE in the quietness for a moment and allow the rose to give of itself to you. Feel the healing power of the flower's beauty.

The rose does not judge your thoughts, words, deeds or who you are; it just gives of its healing power. When you are ill or out of balance, take a moment and ask that the healing energy of a beautiful flower be placed in your hand and allow the flower to give of itself to you.

I embrace you in love, and at this very moment I am extending to you the healing power that exists within my energy. Be open and receive this energy. The healing occurs as your soul opens the doorway to your higher, spiritual essence. Never doubt your beauty or power; simply remain in your own energy of Love.

The more you practice this meditation, the more you will begin to feel the power of who you are. You will not worry about the mundane things of life; they will always be provided. When you flow with your spiritual self, everything in your world is in its perfect place and perfect time for you.

I leave you in the Love that you are, the light and the beauty. I leave you in the Love of the Father that abides eternally in you, and I am Jesus.

PART III

Prophecy

I tell you of the future that your mind may be at ease for there is nothing to fear, your tomorrow holds a bright path of awakening. I will walk with you down this path always so we might experience the glory of divinity together. Fear not anything, for the power and beauty of your Love transforms all things.

—Jesus

CHAPTER 16

Prophecy
- A Time Of Remembrance -

This is Jesus. I come to you in love aware of all of the concerns voiced and experienced by the human soul. It is those concerns I wish to lay to rest. As humanity struggles upon the planet, I wish to say, *all the struggle has no meaning. There is a predestination of remembrance.* Within the predestination there are many choices the human soul can make, but there is not a need to struggle in the present existence of your life. Before your beautiful planet was ever hurled to the far-flung corners of your universe, it was already ingrained with its remembrance of totality and origination.

You are created in the form of this same remembrance. Your human soul experience has all the elements of the planet. Within your physical body you contain the elements, known and unknown, of which your world is made and within that is a memory bank, a path, a road map that takes you home.

And while there are many choices to be made and many paths you may choose, you are all moving in an upward spiral of evolution remembering the original state of perfection in which you were created.

Now what is that original state? In your original state of consciousness, you had no fear. You did not know of good and evil; you had no knowledge there was anything outside yourself. You felt, knew and understood all things were within you. That you, indeed, were the center of your universe and from this center you chose to create many worlds for yourself. But no matter how far you have strayed from that remembrance, you shall always be drawn back to the understanding of your original state of creativity.

So what is happening with planet Earth, and what is taking place within the human soul? There is a great escalation in your awakening, not only to your own expansive individuality but also to your connectedness to the existence of all life. And in the remembrance, you are choosing to find how the individual pieces of your own creativity fit together to make a whole. It's in the expanded awareness that at times you seem to find it difficult to know which path to take.

Yet, I would say to you, see a vision of a mighty cloud of heavenly beings as they travel down a road together having their own individuality but together forming a sense of a continuum of existence. Together they find the right course, steering in the right direction. So it is much like your souls are returning to their original state of being.

Your original state of being recognizes there is no evil in your world, there is no need for struggle, and there is no lack. It is the original state of being in which all was provided for you setting into motion the richness of your existence upon Earth.

Let us go back into the eons of time, and let us talk about when the soul came into existence. The soul came into existence not in a physical form nor was your understanding of life in a physical form. You desired to take physical form, and from the creation of physical form came the third-dimensional form of the planets in your universe by your thought processes.

Your very thought processes brought third-dimensional form from the etheric realm. As this creative process evolved, the elements of those planets also became a part of your own physical form. Your very thought processes brought forth the third-dimensional form containing all knowledge of the Creator. So rest assured that neither your planet nor your soul are separate from the Creator.

Many forms of existence have come and gone since the beginning of time. Your past creations which you do not consciously remember continue to exist. But humanity is beginning to awaken to the awareness all souls are, indeed, eternal beings; all souls, indeed, have a destiny of greatness, and all souls, indeed, are in charge of all they know and all they are.

The human Spirit is beginning to permeate the human soul. Now, let me tell you what I mean by the human Spirit. As you have created from your soul, there is a Spirit level of God consciousness that is not bound by the perceptions and the fears of the soul. This human Spirit continually reaches into the human soul. You may call this human Spirit, your Higher Self or the Holy Spirit. It matters not what you call it. It is the part of you that is the God-essence collectively of soul consciousness. Your individual soul consciousness is beginning to look to the human Spirit to show you the way.

Through religion and rituals, you have reached various levels of understanding Spirit. Whether you call that Spirit God consciousness, Great Spirit, or a named deity it matters not; it is a connection to human Spirit. Now souls are beginning to realize there is a commonalty that runs through all of these searches for the human Spirit. Your ability of worldwide, global communication has expanded your awareness of others.

The more you are able to communicate, the more you find the sameness within the soul; the more you are isolated, the more you search for the differences that are within the soul. The more you find the sameness, the less threatened you feel. The less threatened you feel, the more you begin to recognize there is a loving consciousness in touch with all souls.

You want to call this consciousness God. Too many believe they must look to some unknown, higher source of good. This loving presence is the sustaining energy in all creation. It is the God-essence expressing through the human experience.

Your planet is on a spectacular voyage. You are beginning to search for a greater, common good. Greater unity among humanity will be experienced. You are beginning to realize when you destroy another creation you are destroying yourself as well. All the desire to be destructive, to harm a brother, to destroy your world, will soon begin to fall away. This desire will weaken as the need for safety leaves. The more you begin to recognize the sameness of all souls, the less you fear, and the less you fear, the less you have the need to destroy.

You're beginning to appreciate the different cultures of your brothers and sisters. Many people on your North American continent have come to appreciate the souls who walked before them, the culture of those souls and what they can teach you. This will become more of a worldwide concept. You will begin to see the beauty in the multitude of varied cultures that have been developed, to see the rainbow of all humanity's creations, and to see there is much more that is the same than that which is different.

CHAPTER 17

Prophecy
- A New Community -

As a new day is dawning upon your world, there are some things you can expect to happen. As humanity begins to bond together, a different lifestyle from that which you have known will be required. There will be less need for control. The less need for control will come very slowly, for it will only be as the fear dissipates you will feel safe enough to remove some of your controls.

As events happen on your planet, there will always be those who will attempt to subvert circumstances for their own personal gain, but this attempt for personal gain will only last for short periods of time.

You are becoming a global community and in a global community there is not room for division.

While you may continue to hold individualized styles of living, there will not be division. There will not be any borders closed on your planet. Humanity will be free to travel and move wherever they desire. Communication will be understood by all. A unified communication system will emerge utilizing symbols instead of letters and words.

You will begin to use symbols first in your business community where a symbol means something that is universally known; it has a commonalty to all people. Has this not already begun? The use of symbols will allow all people to understand. This will grow and develop as there is a need to understand global communication.

You are going to have more discoveries in your universe. New planets will be seen and an awareness of other life forms will develop. You are moving toward a greater understanding of the vastness of consciousness as it exists. Remember, you are just a state of consciousness. This is what all creation is; it is a state of consciousness.

If you can think of the Creator as a center of consciousness and that consciousness chooses to explore itself in various ways, you are an exploration of that consciousness. You must think of yourself as God because you are a conscious state of God – God being a state of consciousness, God being consciousness that has intelligence. An intelligent consciousness is what you are.

Your planet is going to undergo times of hardships in some areas. This is because there is resistance to the changes that are taking place. Some individuals are afraid to be free of pain because they fear their own freedom from self-imposed limitation and imprisonment. These individuals will gather together in their own pockets of populations where they may endure famine, war or physical devastation.

There may be rampant disease, physical eruptions within and on the planet, and there may be extreme flooding. Recognize these souls have chosen those circumstances as their particular understanding of who they are at that time. They would feel stripped of their individuality if they were stripped of their pain and their fear, for that is what the ego believes life to be. That is what the ego says makes them alive.

What will happen as you choose to heal your pain and your fear? It is important for you to know you will not lose your individual state of consciousness. It is who you are. You will be no less you than you have ever been, but you will be aware you are so much more. Just as a cell in your body is an individualized consciousness and intelligence within the total of your physical form, you're going to become aware you're a cell in the totality of human Spirit. Within that cell, you have an individual consciousness, the same as the cell in your body, but you can never be separated from the totality of human Spirit. You can never be separate from God which is the consciousness and sustaining force of the universe. It is who you are.

As you begin to allow yourself to trust, you free yourself to step outside of your pain, your fears and your limitations. Your love will become a beacon of light. There will be no question of helping those who have been too afraid to release their pain and fear.

There will be plenty of food to provide for all. There will be beneficial technology for you to enjoy. There will be great artists at work in your world. All will be masters in expression.

There will be a beauty you have not discovered in a very long time. All of nature will begin to reverse the effects that have been placed upon it by your limitations, your fears and your mishandling of your planet.

You will walk upon your planet in the paradise it was always intended to be. This will occur; it is not some promised fantasy. It is not some foretold prophecy that shall never be.

You will not need to lock doors. You will not have a need for health clinics, for you will not have any disease; you will not die of old age.

You will find the animal kingdom in total harmony. You will also find the animal kingdom will be able to survive without killing. You will find some species leaving because they, too, do not choose to live in the harmony of the planet, and, therefore, they will become obsolete and extinct. It is their choice, and they have the right to such a choice. Those species that leave the planet are the part of you that is unwilling to be able to feel secure enough to live without the need to have your own particular, individualized controls in place. Some species will not be comfortable without control.

Now you pose the question as I hear you say, "Well, what will happen then? What happens to us? We and, indeed, most of nature have been used to devouring life to sustain life? What will change? Will there no longer be a need for life to surrender to life to sustain our existence?" The answer is yes. There will not be the need to give life to sustain life. Therefore, there will be an entirely different means of survival on your world. You will find that your food is just simply provided for you by your very thought process, and so it is for the animals as well. The food is not at the expense of another life form. Whatever is needed to sustain your physical is provided by your own thought creation.

The nutrients to sustain your life will all be in energy form. This has been done in the past, and it shall be done again. It was not until the human form chose to take the life of another living thing that you fell from grace, for that was the fall from grace.

The need to sustain existence by taking the existence of another life form began when the human soul felt limited. You no longer understood how to sustain life without feeling threatened by the existence of another life. The very threat of the existence of other life forms gave need for the necessity to extinguish those lives. It brought within you a desire of a carnivorous nature to consume what you believed threatened you. This was, then, the first time there was a need for life to be sustained by the diminishing or the extinguishing of another life.

You first began to sustain your energy by consuming

fruit. Next were the seeds and the vegetables. Then you began to find yourself moving into a greater and greater desire to consume what you did not understand. You did this first through your mind, and you did it second through your physical body. If you did not understand it, you needed to somehow come to understand it by integrating it into yourself, or you needed to destroy it and that became your separation and your fall. Once you felt you no longer were able to sustain your existence and be in harmony with all other existences, you began a journey into fear.

CHAPTER 18

Prophecy
- The Transition -

How shall you return to your total spiritual nature and awareness? You begin by first having a different, more conscious interaction, and connectedness with all life around you. It is then not as easy to have a disregard for other life forms. The connectedness you feel will not allow you to easily extinguish the existence of other life forms, and as this expanded awareness begins to grow, you'll also find your needs and desires are being met with a greater ease and harmony than before. You will feel freer, you will feel lighter, and you will find you have more energy.

Much of your energy today is given to sustaining your existence by having the need of taking the energy of other existences within yourself either to understand it or to consume it. All life will maintain a higher energy as you share your energy together without consuming or destroying another.

Thus, you'll have a higher energy as you begin to have less need for control.

Your skies will be different—more beautiful, clearer at all times. There will be a very gentle rain that comes to moisten your earth. There will not be a need for storms, for the storms are a reflection of the storms within you. There will not be destruction by nature; there will not be volatile forces. There will not be disparity of climates, for all will be in harmony. The four seasons will rotate in a very harmonious manner, and you will find while you may enjoy the various climates and seasons, there will not be the extremes, but rather you will be very comfortable within these climates at all times. There will not be the taking of life nor any discomfort of life. Discomfort with life is only when you are out of harmony with your environmental surroundings.

How is life on the planet meant to be? What is the second coming of Christ? Why do you think my return to the planet would bring harmony? Why do you think that if I returned as some mighty being, I could change your world? Humanity desired I change their world 2,000 years ago. I could not then; I cannot now. I can only help you to change your world.

The second coming of the Christ energy, the Christ Spirit, begins as humanity recognizes that Christ Spirit within themselves and as the individual human soul reaches into the human Spirit for its guidance and Love. That second coming is drawing very near.

Your planet has undergone many changes and shall undergo many more.

However, there is coming a time of reunion with self, a time when the sunsets are even more beautiful and more glorious, a time when the sunrises are very clear, a time when the planet will be pristine in its beauty again. All are coming to that balance and that harmony. A time is coming when there is a place for all life to exist within its own parameters of existence, a time when there is no need for bloodshed, a time when you will understand each other, a time when there will be no lack, no disease, a time of a physical paradise. The time will be very real on your planet.

When it is said to you there are those souls who will enter into heaven and there are those souls who will be admonished, know that heaven is the awareness of who you are and hell is the lack of such an awareness. If there are souls who choose not to awaken and not to become aware of who they are, then they shall live in their own private hell, or the lack of awareness of who they are. They shall live in their chosen, self-imposed prison of limitation. A world of fear shall be their home, and this home will not be your planet. Their home will not be known as your Earth. Your Earth will become the beauty and the brightness of the morning star that it is truly. All shall continue their journey as the souls so choose.

Revelation

Now, I would like to touch very briefly, if I may, on the interpretation of end times by the Christian community.

There shall be an end time, but the end time is not one of judgment. It is one of an era; it is one of a state of consciousness that has lived its experience to the fullest.

In the end state of time or consciousness there shall be instant transformation. A choice must be made to totally relinquish the illusion and release all fears to transformation.

It is a time of total trust and surrender. Those who are willing shall have the experience of instant transformation, and those who are not willing shall not allow instant transformation. It all takes place in the twinkling of an eye and is total and complete within a moment. It shall be instant, and it shall be like living ten billion years of evolution. Suddenly, as you close and open your eyes in a blink, you have come to a new state of awareness, a new state of consciousness, but the transformation can only take place as your freewill allows.

This leap of transformation has taken place on your planet before, that is why you cannot find missing links of evolution. The missing links of evolution were not caused by those of other cultures or other planets interfering with your evolution. The evolution occurred because a critical mass of the then present level of consciousness had completed its expression, and those who were ready moved on to a new state of existence and a new state of consciousness. Only as you are willing to allow the transformation, does it take place.

That's what the end time is about. It's not about your world disappearing, and it's not about sending some souls to a punishment while others are sent to a reward. The reward is simply your allowing the transformation. Perhaps this is what those ancients saw as a heavenly experience but did not know how to explain. Perhaps what they perceived to be the punishment was simply the souls who were not ready to allow the transformation.

If souls over a long period of time do not choose to allow transformation, they shall regress. They shall find their way back into an abyss where they will have time to restructure. This is not punishment; this simply allows the consciousness to make a decision as to how it chooses to continue to evolve into a new state of awareness and consciousness.

Visualize the universal creative source, known as God, as a benevolent, loving parent who allows children complete freedom. This loving, All That Is has given to the child everything it owns and has endowed the child with all its attributes. Compare this to being a parent on Earth. As you have brought forth your children, they have brought forth your genes with the additional capacity to bring forth their own talents and abilities from many lifetimes into this lifetime. You give your children the guidance, the material means, the support and the love so they might be all they choose to be, and that's expressing God consciousness. Just as you might have the ability to take a child from a state of poverty and endow the child with great blessings so the Father can do the same.

Recognize the God consciousness knows when a state of consciousness has completed a particular experience. Transformation takes place. If your child said to you, "I prefer the poverty, I like where I am, I feel safe here, and I'm not really willing to leave this mode of life," then you must respect that individual conscious choice, for you created an individual consciousness endowed with the right of choice. So God gives to you the right of your own choices.

When it has been said one will be taken and one will be left, it is a matter of a soul's choice; it is not because God judges, and it is not because there is a criteria. It is because some let go of fear and are willing to allow the transformation and other souls are not ready. That is now known as your end time.

It is not yet the end time on your planet. You will first have a time of paradise giving all souls the opportunity to experience the grandeur of who they are. A curtain shall open allowing you to view this new and glorious existence. You shall be shown a glorious planet. When that time is over, souls will choose from that point forward—will they allow a transformation to a higher plane or will they still hold to their fears? It is then a soul's choice to live within its higher consciousness. This is when the separation of the sheep from the goats takes place, or a separation of illusion from reality. It is not a matter of judgment; it is the choice of individual soul consciousness. That will be the end time, but it is not for yet.

First there will be a time of paradise. If I say paradise to you, what does it mean? It means to you a world of perfection by whatever your consciousness deems to be perfection. If there happens to be a life form you do not particularly enjoy, perfection might be the absence of that life form. Perhaps perfection to you is to have an abundance of some particular resource or some particular commodity because that's what you have come to equate with an existence in paradise. For one soul paradise might be to live on a tropical island; for another, paradise may be seen as having the autumn experience forever.

So when I speak to you of paradise, I am saying to you, *it is a state of consciousness where all creations are in harmony with All That Is.* But how can you understand that? How can you understand a state of consciousness? You want to have your explanations in a very tangible, a very physical and a very concise, three-dimensional understanding. So I speak to you of paradise in terms of what your consciousness would deem a life as perfection in every way. And I say this to you that you might be able to relate to a time when all will be perfect for you.

Now, for you to enter into paradise is merely to enter into a state of consciousness.

When you enter into a state of consciousness where there is the absence of fear, you are in paradise.

All is beautiful. All is perfect. Sunsets, sunrises are wonderful. Everything is in abundance in your life, for in that state of consciousness you are in the total completeness of joy, love, harmony and peace.

When I speak to you of an eternity without beginning and without ending, how can I convey this understanding to you, who only understand, remember and know of a linear time existence? How can your mind understand no beginning and no ending, an existence that is eternally forever? It is an existence in which you do not have a past or a future. Can you open your understanding to an existence where there is no past and there is no future, where you are eternally living richly and fully in your existence of that particular moment?

CHAPTER 19

Prophecy
- Paradise -

Allow me to go back just one little step with you. At this time in the evolutionary process of human consciousness wherein you exist there is a great amount of turbulence, along with a great amount of searching and seeking for what you have forgotten. For some souls this means to control, manipulate and have power over all others. For others there is a beginning of an awareness there is something more—an awareness that you are a spiritual being who truly contains within your individual consciousness the total and complete universal conscious awareness.

So a great division begins to take place. Now, when I speak to you of paradise, you enter paradise as your consciousness allows you to enter paradise, and as you enter paradise, you are no longer vibrating at a rate that encompasses fear. Thus, you enter into a state of consciousness where everything you know today exists, but it exists in total and perfect harmony.

Paradise is not something that happens because the planet is washed clean. It's an existence that comes into being as individualized consciousness creates it to be.

As you exist in that state of being, you are just as real in your physical sense as you are today. But it's an entirely different state of consciousness. The consciousness of paradise is preparing you to see and understand your God consciousness—the truth of who you truly are. All souls are being given the opportunity to enter into this state of consciousness known as paradise.

Paradise will still contain a remembrance and an awareness of those souls who have not yet obtained such a state of consciousness, but you'll not feel pain because of this awareness. You'll only recognize this level of existence has been a freewill choice by those souls. You shall have no judgments. All human souls have complete freedom to choose Love or fear, reality or illusion. In time, all will choose Love.

You will also choose to assist those souls in reaching a higher vibration, a higher state of consciousness by loving them, by teaching them, by showing them the way to remember. And when that time comes to an end, so it is the end time. At the end time there will be transformation.

The transformation will occur because you have allowed yourself to accelerate into a higher state of eternal, now consciousness where there is no fear or limitation. Out of eternal, now consciousness will come new creativity, new experiences, new expressions, and so it shall forever be.

When you see a fireworks exploding and its rays of beauty shine brightly, you know it lasts for only a brief moment. Then a newness must follow, another new explosion, another new experience and expression. The vibration changes and the existence changes to a new and different form of an experience and expression. You must simply allow this understanding to unfold for you because the analytical mind has nothing to relate to in its present memory.

You are in a time of the acceleration of awareness. Many will begin to step into this time of paradise which will be a very real, third-dimensional experience. But the time will also come, as it has before, when you will have the individualized, expressive choice of going into transformation or remaining in a controlled ego.

Just because you are experiencing paradise does not mean you recognize the total perfection of life. Experiencing paradise gives you the opportunity for this recognition. Paradise is a time to experience unity and expanded consciousness. Souls will unite in harmony at this time, and you are a part of that experience.

If you listen to my words, know you have chosen to be a part of the experience. You are choosing to be a standard bearer bringing light to your world by dispelling the darkness of fear. You are dispelling the myths of human bondage. You are bringing to the world an enlightenment that allows each soul to reach to the greatest heights it desires.

As the time draws near, the pageant is presented, all the players are in place, and the whole world will be the stage. The whole world will take part in the drama. When the great pageantry of this era of consciousness closes, then shall be the end time. Then will come the division by the souls' choice. But not before everyone, every soul has had an opportunity to know the great Love of the Creator, to know that all creations are created in the image of a very loving, and benevolent Creator.

Q: We've had other experiences before, so we're never left behind I guess, and we will experience something new again; it's just transformation. We are never eliminated. We just continually go on with different experiences, right?

You are an individualized consciousness that shall always exist with the exception of a relinquishment by your freewill of the individual process because you no longer choose it, but it will never be taken from you. There are those souls who feel they have experienced and expressed in every way they choose, and they wish to relinquish the individuality. For a soul to relinquish its individuality is possible but not something that is ever taken from you.

Q: The Bible states that paradise will exist for 1,000 years and since time is collapsing, there won't literally be 1,000 years—so, when our consciousness reaches the state of paradise, will that "time" be whatever "time" it takes for each person to reach that point?

But does not your scriptures say 1,000 years is as a day and a day is as 1,000 years? It is an attempt to say to you time has no meaning.

Q: Will every soul that has ever incarnated on planet Earth, the third-dimensional experience, be given the opportunity to be in this paradise, to see what it is like in this paradise, and then to make that decision?

Yes. Every soul shall be given the opportunity. You must recognize your present state of limitation and choose expansion of your consciousness. Many shall so choose. Many shall leave this time of limitation and enter into the state of consciousness of paradise and in paradise there is no limitation. However, as always, it is a freewill choice of each soul.

Q: Are there souls now that are not in physical incarnations that could incarnate into paradise now?

Not at this time. You are beginning to enter that level of awareness once again as a collective consciousness. Those individual souls who have a greater awareness presently have not entered paradise, for, indeed, you are presently creating that level of existence by collectively awakening.

Q: Jesus, what would you say to the people concerning the whole core of the philosophy that Jesus died for our sins and it's the only way to return to God?

It is my hope that my presence among you says more than the words. Life is complex. Creation is not a simple process. But if you remember to love, if you remember your soul is in pain as are other souls, you can free your soul as you love, so it is then you bring healing to your world. If you remember love is All That Is, you begin to walk upon the road to your salvation, your road to peace, your road to joy and eternal bliss.

You must have love and understanding for those who seek their salvation in a structured way—a way they understand—for they choose to have set rules. These souls often seek direction from others not recognizing the power and Love within their own souls. They have come to see their religion as being able to place their faith in what they do not understand. Such souls feel they must have something stronger than themselves. And for them it is now their path.

All souls shall come to know the reality of Love that is, indeed, their own salvation. I would say to them, and I would say to you, *love one another. For as you love one another and as you judge not one another, so you free not only yourself but your brother and sister.* It's a simple message. It's the answer to your understanding of life, to freeing yourself from your fears and to moving back into the awareness of your God consciousness.

I am totally aware of all the churches, restrictions, and rules you have imposed upon yourself. I stand back, and I give my love and that is what you must do.

I am not greater than you. I bow my knee to you, for as you go through your experiences and your existence on your world, you truly seek to find what deep within your soul you already know. I am grateful for those who help to light the way, for you are the light of the world, and you dispel the darkness. I will help you.

I will be there; I will walk by your side as do many. But the words can only be spoken, and the souls must choose. Just as it was in eons past, just as it was when I was on your planet and just as it is today, so shall it always be. The word will be spoken, but the souls must choose.

Let me give to each of you a moment of blessing, for you are dear and precious to my heart. I convey to you from my Spirit to your Spirit great love. I want to wrap your wounds. I want to take away the pain. I want to sit and cry with you through the night until the daylight comes. I want you to see the glory that you are.

Join in the beauty of the sunrise, the peacefulness of the sunset. And as the sun rises and as the sun sets, so it shall always be. There shall always be beginnings and there shall always be endings, but they all exist within the eternal now moment, for in truth there is no beginning and there is no ending. I walk with you always in love; I am Jesus.

A Final Word From Jesus

Anew day is dawning, bringing new meaning to your world and your life. I give this message to your world today to bring clarity and inspiration in a time when confusion reigns.

As a collective consciousness, you feel the uncertainty of your time. You are traveling on a path of remembrance. Whenever there is a great paradigm shift in mass consciousness, it always brings forth a grand explosion of God expressing in a new and expanded beauty of brilliance and grandeur. And so it is. Your souls are emerging from the shadow of illusion, pain and fear into the daylight of Love, truth and reality. My love is with you always. I walk by your side as you journey into your tomorrow.

—Jesus

About the Author

Diandra is an internationally-known, spiritual teacher, retreat leader and personal consultant. In 1986 Diandra left a successful career in finance to dedicate her life to full-time spiritual service. In 1993 Diandra and Batavia, her soul mate, co-founded Inward Journey - Gateway to Expansion, an organization dedicated to helping others find and live their inner truth. Inward Journey maintains a base in both the Midwest and the Southwest part of the United States in which both Diandra and Batavia are very active.

Diandra joins with others in this organization to bring the message of remembrance that we are Love. Those whose lives she touches feel her love for others, this planet and all of life.

Diandra spent much of her younger life with missionary grandparents under whose guidance she developed a personal relationship with Jesus at a young age. This deep spiritual part of her life would prepare her to receive the message in this book.

In 1980 Diandra was involved in an automobile accident that left her in bed with a back injury for 14 months. During that time her constant search was for a deeper understanding of God, truth and the meaning of life. This search led to months of prayer, meditation and continuous questions to God.

Although Diandra had been a lifelong student of the Bible and had maintained an active role in her church, this "time out" in her life brought a new awareness of our relationship with our Creator. It was a slow journey through her own questions and fears that finally led to a place of true peace and inner knowing that allowed her to feel God's love fully. Her surrender and trust gave way to a powerful new awareness that God is Love and that we are the expression of a loving Creator. This was a turning point in her life, as the many hours spent in this spiritual journey would ultimately lead her life in a new direction.

About The Inward Journey Organization

Inward Journey-Gateway to Expansion is an organization founded in 1993 by Diandra and Batavia. Their deep desire to help people find and live their inner truth is the foundation of the organization. Batavia is a public speaker, writer and teacher. Together their dedication and talents have spawned a dynamic organization designed to meet the needs in the lives of people today.

Inward Journey assists you on your journey of self-discovery through live events, experiential workshops, enjoyable retreats, books, video and audiocassettes. We provide you with the tools to discover your inner source of power that contains the solutions for life's everyday challenges.

You may see this personal quest as your spiritual journey, personal growth, or a search for self-awareness as you seek a higher meaning to life. No matter what you may call your path of self-discovery, Inward Journey is an organization created and designed for the sole purpose of empowering and supporting you on your path leading to a life filled with joy, love, beauty, peace and your own self-empowerment.

To receive a free catalog of current products, including audiocassette programs by Diandra, or if you would like a free information packet about the Inward Journey organization, or to order another copy of this book, please call or write to the location nearest you:

Inward Journey   Inward Journey
P.O. Box 6418   P.O. Box 239
Naperville, IL 60567-6418   Sedona, AZ 86339-0239

1-888-980-5780

To learn more about Inward Journey, visit our website at:
http://www.inwardjourney.com

About Diandra's Personal Consultations

A personal consultation with Diandra is available in person or by phone. Diandra gives you insight into the important issues in your life today, as well as the effect of your past lives upon this life. You gain clarity that can help when you are in transition or looking for direction or purpose in your life. You gain valuable insight and clear understanding about yourself, the relationships in your life and your current situation which can offer guidance when you are making important decisions. The future direction of your life is explored. Your questions are answered with accuracy.

Diandra has helped thousands of people all over the world find clarity and direction in their lives. Clients consistently comment on the accuracy, professionalism and empowering nature of her consultations. The consultation is recorded on tape for your future reference.

**MasterCard and Visa are Accepted.
Call 1-888-578-8090 today for more information or to schedule an appointment with Diandra by phone or in person.**

Index